From Nashborough
to the Nobel Prize

The Buchanans of Tennessee

Copyright © 2012 Jeff Whorley
All rights reserved

This book may not be reproduced or transmitted, in whole or in part, through any means electronic or mechanical, including photocopying or electronic transmission, without prior written permission from the author, except short excerpts considered normal for review.

ISBN 978-1-937937-03-4

First Edition

Printed in the United States of America

Twin Oaks Press
twinoakspress@gmail.com
www.twinoakspress.com

Cover and interior design
By Sally Ham Govan

Cover photography: front, Tennessee State Library and Archives; back: top, Tennessee State Library and Archives; middle, George Mason University; bottom: *Nashville Banner*, Nashville Public Library

From
Nashborough
to the Nobel Prize

The Buchanans of Tennessee

by Reuben Kyle

with Kevin H. Cason

TWIN
OAKS
PRESS

Table of Contents

Foreword		1
I.	Introduction	7
II.	The Buchanan Family in North America	23
III.	The 2nd Generation: Buchanans of the 19th Century	65
IV.	Buchanans and the Civil War	75
V.	John Price Buchanan and the Agrarian Revolt	105
VI.	The Buchanan Family in the 20th Century	161
VII.	James M. Buchanan Jr.	197
VIII.	Epilogue	211
Bibliography		215
Figures		233
Index		235
Appendix A	The Political Economy of James M. Buchanan	237
Appendix B	Buchanan Family Genealogy	257

This book is dedicated

to the memory

of James McGill Buchanan.

ACKNOWLEDGMENTS

As is usually the case of any work of nonfiction, this book is the product of the efforts of many people. The idea for the preparation of a book on the Buchanan family was inspired by a donation from the family to the James E. Walker Library at Middle Tennessee State University (MTSU) for the purpose of endowing a reading room in that facility to honor the only MTSU graduate to receive a Nobel Prize, James M. Buchanan Jr., and his antecedents. Buchanans have made significant contributions to middle Tennessee, the university, and the intellectual resources of the world.

For my part, the first word of thanks must go to my colleagues Barbara S. Haskew and Robert B. Jones, who recommended me to the sponsors of this project. I am flattered and honored by their confidence in me.

Most important among the contributors to this work are the members of the Buchanan family, Dr. James M. Buchanan, Elizabeth Buchanan Bradley, and John F. Whorley Jr. Dr. Buchanan was extremely generous with his time and energy in submitting to several interview sessions and with advice on much of the material both on his family and on his work. Unfortunately, he did not live to see the book in print. Liz Bradley likewise was most helpful in participating in interviews and keeping this writer on the path of truth and accuracy. Jeff Whorley provided the inspiration and supported the research for this project. Without his efforts this project would never have been accomplished. It was my pleasure and honor to come to know them and be a part of the production of the history of their remarkable family.

In addition to their role in involving me in the project, both Barbara Haskew and Bob Jones read the manuscript and offered many valuable suggestions. Major editorial support was provided by John R. Vile, dean of the University Honors College, who added much to the manuscript as well as guidance in the process of developing a publishable work. Others who read all or parts of the manuscript and offered more valuable editorial advice include Francis R. Ginanni, Anne D. Taylor, Robert L. Taylor, and Connie L. Lester. Many thanks go to them for their time and encouraging editorial advice. Special thanks for the many hours Ron Messier and June McCash spent in reading and offering suggestions and comments on several versions of the manuscript. Finally, the contributions of Kevin Cason warranted the addition of his name to the cover of this book. His scholarship as evidenced here certainly presages a productive career as an academician and historian.

For assistance with the research invested in the project, I benefited greatly from the help of John Lodl and his staff of the Rutherford County, Tennessee, Archives; Rick Warwick of the Heritage Foundation of Franklin and Williamson County, Tennessee; the staff of the Williamson County, Tennessee, Archives; Judy Williams, the special collections librarian of the Lila D. Bunch Library at Belmont University; and the staff of the Tennessee State Library and Archives. This work would never have been completed without the enthusiastic support and diligent research of Josh Alexander, who was indispensable to this project.

Don Craig, dean emeritus of the MTSU Walker Library, and Bill Black of the library staff, who supervised the project from the outset, have provided wonderful support for my efforts and encouraged me at every turn. In 2011, MTSU celebrated its centennial. This work salutes the Buchanan family members who contributed to its history and burnish the reputation of this institution.

During the final year of producing this volume Sally Ham Govan has taught me a great deal about writing as well as the art of publishing. In addition to designing the book, she has been my editor and mentor. I owe many thanks for her diligence and her patience.

Finally, I would like to thank my wife, Carroll T. Kyle, who read many drafts of the manuscript, traveled many miles during the conduct of the research, and visited many cemeteries in search of Buchanan forebearers.

—Reuben Kyle

FOREWORD

BY BARBARA HASKEW

I first met James Buchanan in the mid-1960s when I attended a month-long seminar on the University of Virginia campus. Buchanan and other professors from UVA and the University of Chicago lectured and led discussions on contemporary economic topics. On most afternoons the faculty and seminar participants gathered for some libation in a more comfortable and interactive surrounding. Early in the program Buchanan introduced himself for the purpose of discussing our common Tennessee roots. I remember thinking that he was the most elegant and gracious man I had ever met.

At that time Buchanan was already at the height of his academic powers. He had published (with coauthor Gordon Tullock) *The Calculus of Consent* in 1962, a work central to the creation of the field of public choice. In the preface to the book, Buchanan notes that the focus of this work "lies squarely along that mythical and mystical borderline" between the disciplines of economics and politics. It is there that Buchanan and Tullock attempt "to analyze the calculus of the rational individual when he is faced with questions of constitutional choice." More than 35 years later, in the preface to a second publication of the book, Robert D. Tollison concluded:

> The Calculus *is a radical book. It is a radical departure from the way politics is analyzed, and it carries within its methodological framework the seeds of a radical departure in the way democracies conduct their business.* The Calculus *is already a book for the ages.*

Understanding the forces that influenced Buchanan and his academic contributions is best accomplished by reading his memoir, *Better Than Plowing*. In discussing his journey to the award of the 1986 Nobel Memorial Prize in Economic Sciences, Buchanan emphasized that his path was not strewn with the wealth and privilege that opened doors to the nation's premier educational institutions. In the depths of the Great Depression, his dream of attending Vanderbilt University shrank to attending State Teachers College at Murfreesboro as a day student. Moreover, the economic needs of the family farm required him to eschew extracurricular activities in order to milk the cows and undertake other farm chores, but Buchanan learned from the hard work his economic circumstances required. He may have carried a few scars associated with the opportunity costs attached to those tasks, but they also became badges of honor and independence for him. Buchanan believed that students may learn from his experiences and accomplishments and be motivated to chart their own paths designed to explore and develop their potential.

In developing the information for this book, researchers took a deep dive into the family's genealogy. They searched the sturdy Scotch-Irish roots and experiences of his forebears for behavior and accomplishments that may have contributed to Buchanan's tenacity and boldness as well as his pioneering intellectual approaches. As the author of this book was pursuing Buchanan's roots in historical documents and graveyards, I sometimes had the opportunity to tag along. One of these trips took us to the Tennessee State Archives as we tracked the path of the Buchanan clan from Pennsylvania to the North Carolina frontier that would later become Tennessee. My favorite of these early ancestors was James Buchanan's great-great grandfather, who was already a seasoned pioneer and frontier warrior at the age of 22 when he created *John Buchanan's Book of Arithmetic* in 1781. History records that he killed a deer and dressed its hide to provide a substantial cover for the small book. A graceful rendering of flowers on the cover (see page 44) testifies to Buchanan's artistic skills and appreciation of beauty. The small schoolbook served to provide both the proofs of basic mathematical operations and calculations necessary for commerce on the frontier. One of the treasures of the archives, it is carefully maintained in a refrigerator. We had to put on white gloves just to hold it in our hands as we considered its impact on the remote frontier in the nation's earliest years.

Better Than Plowing notes Buchanan's pride in his grandfather, John Price Buchanan, a livestock farmer in Rutherford County whose political leadership on agricultural issues propelled him into the governor's chair in 1891. This legacy continued to produce stature for the family long after the governor's term ended, and Buchanan grew up on the family farm in the community of Gum sensing the continued influence and respect produced by his grandfather's political career. Although the work required on the family farm was physical and hard, Buchanan had time to dream, which made the hard work bearable. He recalls imagining himself in high political office, controlling crowds with both powerful ideas and extraordinary oratory. Perhaps some vestige of those power-filled daydreams contributed to his later focus on the intersection of economic tools and political decision-making.

Another of my favorite excursions was visiting James Buchanan at his home in the rolling Virginia countryside. The two cozy houses and the massive fir trees that shelter them date well back into another century. Selected quotations of famous economists and philosophers that held special significance for him ornament the walls of one room. It is a secluded and simple working farm that provided the opportunity for him to use the practical agricultural skills learned in his early years. It is easy to imagine that the songs Buchanan wrote to endure long hours of plowing as a teenager were later replaced with more philosophical and complex musings or just by the enjoyment of simple tasks performed in his own domain.

On this visit we had the opportunity to see and hold the Nobel medallion. Buchanan was full of energy and good cheer, and when we all went in search of dinner at a local restaurant, he casually dropped the prize into his pants pocket. Almost like a practiced mother, I worried about such casual treatment of so important a trophy. Of course, the real and continuing value of the Nobel Prize resides in the recognition of Buchanan's work, the understandings mined in that fertile fence row between two academic fields and the further ideas that it may produce from future scholars.

For more than 40 years, James Buchanan visited the MTSU campus and lectured on economics and ideas for improving higher education. His intellectual work continues to command attention as democratic societies around the globe search for solutions in constitutional processes and policies to address massive budget deficits and high unemployment. The university and the state of Tennessee honor Buchanan's extraordinary accomplishments with a marker at the center of the MTSU campus. It is the type of marker usually placed on the side of a highway to commemorate a famous homeplace or a great event. The Buchanan marker, however, is strategically placed so that students walking to classes or the library cannot fail to notice it. It reads in part:

> *James McGill Buchanan, economist and author, received the 1986 Nobel Memorial Prize in Economic Sciences. Grandson of a former governor, he attended Middle Tennessee State Teachers College, the University of Tennessee, and the University of Chicago. Buchanan's emphasis on applying market principles to political choice led to the founding of the sub-discipline of Public Choice, recognized throughout the world.*

Middle Tennessee State University and James Buchanan hoped that the students who paused to read the words on the marker would be motivated by his example to have bigger dreams, aspire to greater heights, and work harder. Reflecting on his southern roots and his independent path to extraordinary intellectual accomplishment, he told MTSU students, "If a boy from Gum,

Tennessee, can win a Nobel Prize, then maybe you can, too."

Barbara Haskew, economics faculty emeritus and former provost of Middle Tennessee State University, serves on the Tennessee Valley Authority Board of Directors.

CHAPTER I.

INTRODUCTION

This is the story of the Buchanan family of Tennessee, a story that in many respects mirrors the history of the country but culminates in an accomplishment that few achieve. Like many of the European settlers of North America, the Buchanans' story begins in Scotland, moves to Ireland, and crosses the Atlantic. It follows the family as it settles a dangerous and difficult new world, helps build a community and society in mid-19th century America, survives the brutal Civil War and the challenging years after that conflict, and thrives in the 20th century. The title *From Nashborough to the Nobel Prize* refers to the path of a Buchanan family member, James McGill Buchanan Jr., who was not a political figure or a businessman like others of the family but a scholar and teacher. Still, he was representative of the hardworking, independent-minded family, even the prototypical American family, from which he came.

On October 16, 1986, James McGill Buchanan Jr. was named the recipient of the Nobel Prize in Economics. His work is described as a bridge between economics and political science, an application of the tools of economics to public or collective decision-making. The announcement stated the following.

> *The Royal Swedish Academy of Sciences has decided to award the 1986 Alfred Nobel Memorial Prize in Economic Sciences to Professor James McGill Buchanan, George Mason University, Virginia, USA, for his development of the contractual and constitutional bases for the theory of economic and political decision-making.*
>
> *... Traditional economic theory explains in great detail how consumers and entrepreneurs make decisions regarding purchase of goods, choice of work, production, investments, etc. In a series of studies, Buchanan has developed a corresponding theory of decision-making in the public sector.*[1]

Rather than speak of a branch or a field of economics, Buchanan liked to describe his interests as his research program. Today that program is known as *public choice*. One of the foundations of public choice is that decisions, even in collective settings or governments, are made by individuals whose behavior is determined by their assessment of their own interests. In other words, the decision-makers make choices by analyzing the benefits and costs to themselves of the alternatives they face in finding agreement with others involved in the decision process. The approach differs from other work in public decision-making that assumes a single or aggregated decision maker—a dictator, benevolent or not. Buchanan himself has described public choice as "politics without romance."²

As might be expected of a Nobel laureate, Buchanan's work is challenging for those who are not specialists in the field. At this point we address the question of who the man was and save a more extensive discussion of his work until later in the book.

Nonacademics think of academics as leading an easy existence, teaching only a few hours a week and enjoying many holidays. While it is true that a college professor teaches classes for only a few hours each week, the dedicated teacher spends many hours interacting with students and in preparation for the few hours spent lecturing. A scholar such as James Buchanan devotes many more hours to reading, research, and writing. Preparing and writing scholarly books and articles is usually a long, challenging process. The time span from an idea's conception to its final acceptance for publication may be many months, possibly even years. More months or years may transpire until the accepted piece appears in print.

In the case of James Buchanan, the products of his efforts are truly staggering. Between 1951 and 2011, he wrote or coauthored 39 books. At age 90, he continued to write and publish. In addition, he published nearly 300 significant articles in the most prestigious academic journals in the world, including the *American Economic Review*, *Journal of Political Economy*, and *Quarterly Journal of Economics*, to name only a few. The process for publishing in academic journals is usually highly competitive: a group of readers review each submitted paper, typically without knowing the author's name, and many more papers are submitted than can be published. Among the top journals in economics, only about one of every 10 papers is accepted for publication.

This impressive record of work does not include material in books edited by others, book reviews, or reviews of others' work in progress. It also does not include the invited lectures delivered in every corner of the globe, the hours spent supervising students' theses and dissertations, or the myriad administrative activities in which any college faculty member is expected to participate. An academician's job typically is not physically demanding, but Buchanan's work habits would challenge anyone in any occupation as demonstrated by his prodigious output.

Clearly one facet of this man's character was his dedication and devotion to his work. A colleague and collaborator pointed out that, during his most active years, James Buchanan began his work day at 6 a.m. and continued until about 5:30 p.m. Monday through Saturday and worked at least half of Sunday. Buchanan replied, "I became convinced that somehow if I worked harder that it had to provide a benefit," not just to himself but to the economy.[3]

One benefit of his devotion to scholarship is found in what he described as "pure serendipity," his discovery of a small book that provided an important direction to his life and work. After completing his own dissertation at the University of Chicago, while waiting to report to his first job, he was browsing in the university library and found a copy of a dissertation by a notable Swedish economist, Knut Wicksell. The dissertation was written in German, a language that Buchanan had studied for an examination required in his own Ph.D. program. On reading the book he found ideas that coincided with his own notions about taxation and government finance. At that point he decided to translate the book into English. It was a decision that set the path for the rest of his career.[4]

While spending the early years of his teaching life at the University of Tennessee and then at Florida State University, with a year in Italy on a Fulbright fellowship along the way, Buchanan established himself as a rising young scholar. He then moved to the University of Virginia in Charlottesville. At one point in those early years, he was invited to join the faculty at one of the most prestigious economics departments in the world, the University of Chicago, but he says "I'm glad that I didn't." By choosing institutions less in the academic limelight, he was able to establish his own reputation. "It has allowed me to work somewhat more independently, to develop my own ideas rather than in a cocoon of people who were so dominant that they would have made it difficult for me to be as independent."[5]

Those choices along with other aspects of his background encourage him to tell students and other scholars, "If I can get a Nobel Prize, you can get a Nobel Prize." He enjoyed making that statement at lesser-known universities because he found that it "energizes the people."[6] This attitude about his place in the academic world does not indicate a lack of confidence in his abilities but is one more testament to his independent mind and recognition of his rise from rather humble beginnings.

He began his serious study of economics following World War II. A child of the Great Depression, he said he arrived at the University of Chicago as a socialist, like many of that generation. However, after encountering one of his lifelong mentors, Professor Frank Knight, he became a committed advocate of free markets. That inclination led him to a preference for a limited government with its role defined by a constitution. As a result he was often categorized as a political conservative, an issue he addressed in his book *Why I, Too, Am Not a Conservative*.[7] Here he explained that he is a classical liberal as opposed to a conservative or a modern liberal.

A thorough discussion of the complexities of philosophical and political thought is beyond the scope of this book. First, the terms conservative and liberal can be defined only within a given context. In Buchanan's work the terms apply to modern Western views of human society. He was anxious to distinguish his own views as a classical liberal, such as Adam Smith, from those of conservatives, though the two have often been allied in policy debates. The conservative and the modern liberal both view people as inherently unequal. The conservative, in favoring the status quo, sees inequality as a natural hierarchy, perhaps ameliorated by rules to deter bad behavior and promote good behavior. A modern liberal sees inequality as a motivation for policies to reduce inequality. By contrast, a classical liberal sees all people as equal—not in physical, mental, or social endowments—but in the right to choose their own actions. In simple terms, the distinction between a classical liberal and a conservative is that the latter prefers to protect the status quo while the former is open to change. The distinction between a classical liberal and a modern liberal is that the former advocates a limited, clearly defined role for government while the latter advocates a more active, interventionist government. However, simply applying labels to Buchanan's views hardly does him justice.[8]

First and foremost James Buchanan was a scholar. He said he had no interest in "saving the world." In his view economists are engaged in a process, a dialogue, "a sort of constitutional convention, so to speak," in which improving the world is a possible goal, but not improving it in a way that satisfies one person's view of a better world.[9]

He had great antipathy for discrimination and for those who benefit from status they have not earned on their own merit. As a result he said that if he had been born outside the United States he would have been a socialist. In the United States there are fewer impediments to upward mobility than in Europe, where social status is far more important. For example, Britain has much more social stratification than the United States. He noted that an Italian friend who has been a socialist all his life would be a libertarian if he had been born in the United States. Growing up in different environments affects one's view of the world.[10]

What environment produced this particular man? James McGill Buchanan Jr. was born on October 3, 1919, to James McGill Buchanan and Lila Herrin Scott Buchanan on the Buchanan farm south of Murfreesboro in Rutherford County, Tennessee. His father managed the family farm that his grandfather, John Price Buchanan, left without designating the distribution of the property among his many children. Mother Lila had been a schoolteacher before her marriage and assumed the role of family teacher.

In his autobiography, *Economics from the Outside In: "Better than Plowing" and Beyond*, Buchanan relates the story of his childhood on the farm.[11] From the time he was a child until he left to enter graduate school at the University of Tennessee in Knoxville in the fall of 1940, Jim Buchanan shared the farm work. He describes life on the farm:

> *There was work: plowing, manuring, harrowing, planting, cultivating, hoeing, haying, threshing, picking, milking, herding, feeding—work for long hours on days during growing seasons and in weather foul and fair throughout the year.*[12]

The Buchanan farmhouse was typical of the Southern farm of the 1920s with no pretense of luxury, but he also remembered books, magazines, and family discussions at the dinner table that were probably not typical of the homes of his neighbors. From an early age he discovered a passion for learning. His mother supervised his education and supplemented it when she felt it necessary. As a result he entered school already reading and completed high school by the age of 16.

Dreams of attending Vanderbilt University disappeared with the worsening economic conditions of the Depression years of the 1930s.[13] As a result young Jim Buchanan entered State Teachers College, Murfreesboro, as a day student in the fall of 1936, before his 17th birthday. He commuted every day to school and back to the farm, usually with a Methodist minister who was trying to finish his own degree while preaching. In retrospect Buchanan viewed his commuting as beneficial since it prohibited his participation in the usual college social scene. Lacking the distractions of campus life, he concentrated on his studies, and he completed three majors: English, mathematics, and social science.

Among those at the college who most influenced Jim's future was Dr. C. C. Sims, a faculty member and later head of the social science department, which included the economics courses offered. Sims had earned a Ph.D. from the University of Chicago only a few years earlier, and he infused the young Buchanan with the idea that Chicago was a campus full of intellectual fervor. Later, Jim would recall that enthusiasm and follow his mentor's lead.

After graduating in 1940 from the Teachers College, as it was called by students of the era, Jim's options as he later recalled them were to work in a bank or to take a fellowship at the University of Tennessee. When he was asked what inspired him to study economics, he replied:

> *Well, that's a very simple answer. That was the only area that I could get a fellowship in, pure and simple. At the Teachers College, I had three majors. I had a major in mathematics; I had a major in English Literature; I had a major in the social sciences. They didn't have enough economics. They had a couple of courses. So I had very limited job opportunities in 1939, 1940. Dr. Sims, the one who taught the social sciences courses, knew there was a fellowship [in economics] at the University of Tennessee, and so I applied for the fellowship and got the fellowship for $50 a month. Had it been in mathematics, I would have been a mathematician. Had it been in literature, I would have been a literary critic.*[14]

Once again, at the University of Tennessee as at State Teachers College, there was one faculty member who made a positive impression on the young man. Jim took a course in research methods from Professor Charles P. White and served as his graduate assistant. White's work habits and dedication to his work impressed Jim. Toward the end of his year in Knoxville, he again faced the choice of his next direction. A faculty member in statistics helped Buchanan obtain the offer of a graduate assistantship in the Ph.D. program in statistics at Columbia University in New York City, but the prospect of war impacted the course of his education with great consequences for the field of economics.

Facing the virtual certainty of being drafted, Jim Buchanan elected to enter a Navy officer training program on the Columbia University campus in New York City. He recalls in *Better Than Plowing* that in the final months of that training the Japanese bombed Pearl Harbor, Hawaii, where the United States had military bases, which resulted in another of the major influences on his future. On completing the training course, he and seven other newly commissioned ensigns were assigned to the Naval College in Newport, Rhode Island, for further specialized training.

There he received a personal lesson in discrimination. Many among his fellow officers were southerners. Organized alphabetically, it turned out that his group included no one from the Ivy League or other elite eastern schools, so the Navy school instructors moved one such cadet into his group to be the leader. Since fewer than 10 percent of the young men were from Ivy League schools, this snub infuriated him. It was a lesson he remembered the rest of his life, though not with bitterness.

When he finished the six weeks in Rhode Island, he received orders to report to the staff of Admiral Chester Nimitz, commander-in-chief, Pacific (CINCPAC), in Pearl Harbor. Nimitz, a World War II icon, received good, though not perfect, reviews by the former young naval officer. Buchanan worked for the one-time chief of staff and later deputy commander for Nimitz, Admiral Raymond Spruance, who later became a naval hero in his own right. Admiral Spruance once introduced his subordinate in the following manner: "This is Buchanan, who is mighty fast and fairly accurate." Buchanan would jest that he always thought *Mighty Fast and Fairly Accurate* would be the perfect title for his autobiography, but instead he chose *Better Than Plowing*.[15]

One interesting story from his wartime years concerns his only time serving on a warship. At one point during his assignment at the Naval headquarters, a superior officer thought the young reserve officers working there should experience life on board. As it happened Buchanan was assigned to the cruiser *U.S.S. Indianapolis*, where he once again served on the staff of Admiral Spruance. During his limited time on the ship, he witnessed the assault on Kwajalein Atoll in the Marshall Islands and experienced the cruiser firing its guns during the bombardment of the island. It was a first-hand taste of actual naval combat. He was on the *Indianapolis* for some weeks and then returned to his regular duties at Pearl Harbor. After Buchanan's departure the *U.S.S. Indianapolis* entered the history books by fulfilling a historic mission: it was the vessel that transported the nuclear bomb dropped on Nagasaki, Japan, on August 9, 1945. On its return to the Philippines from the island of Saipan, the ship was sunk by a Japanese submarine.[16] Of the 1,196 men on the ship, only 316 survived: almost 600 died of wounds, exposure, and shark attacks. Buchanan knew many of those who died.[17]

Following the war's conclusion in October 1945, Buchanan married Anne Bakke, whom he had met two years earlier at Hickam Field, Oahu, Hawaii. Anne had served as a nurse with the Army Air Transport Command. Jim Buchanan was released from active duty in November 1945.

On leaving the Navy, Buchanan took advantage of the G.I. Bill, which offered returning veterans U.S. government funds to go to college. The seed planted by Dr. C. C. Sims at Teachers College back in Murfreesboro came to fruition. Buchanan enrolled in the graduate program in economics at the University of Chicago in the winter quarter of 1946. While at Chicago, Jim Buchanan associated with teachers and fellow students who became some of the most renowned American economists of the 20th century.

Here again, one teacher, Professor Frank Knight, influenced him more than any other. Knight had followed an academic path similar to Buchanan's. He began his higher education in a small Tennessee college, Milligan College in the northeast corner of the state, then moved on to the University of Tennessee, and finally earned a Ph.D. degree, in his case at Cornell University. Buchanan credits his mentor, Knight, with transforming him into an economist.[18]

On completing his degree in 1948, Jim accepted his first academic job at the University of Tennessee. After three years in Knoxville, he moved to Florida State University, where he stayed until accepting a Fulbright Fellowship to study at the University of Rome for a year. During this year spent in Italy, 1955–1956, he immersed himself in the field of public finance, the subdiscipline of economics devoted to the study of government expenditures and taxation. He regarded this experience as providing the foundation for the work that ultimately led him to receive the 1986 Nobel

Prize in Economic Science.

Clearly James Buchanan was his own man. By his own initiative he transformed himself from a Tennessee farm boy into a renowned scholar. Despite beginning his studies at what were then rather modest institutions of higher education, he earned a doctorate from one of the world's great universities. Later in this book we will examine the intellectual history and contributions of James Buchanan. At this point we retrace the fascinating path his family followed to the point where one among their number achieved this highest of intellectual honors, a Nobel Prize.

Notes

1. "The Prize in Economics 1986—Press Release," October 16, 1986, Nobelprize.org, retrieved from *http://nobelprize.org/nobel_prizes/economics/laureates/1986/press.html*, April 9, 2012.

2. James M. Buchanan, "Public Choice: The Origins and Development of a Research Program," Public Choice Society, retrieved from *http://www.pubchoicesoc.org/about_pc.html*, November 28, 2006.

3. Geoffrey Brennan, *A Conversation with James M. Buchanan*, Parts 1 and 2 (Liberty Fund, Inc., 2001) (DVD).

4. James M. Buchanan, *Better than Plowing and Other Personal Essays* (Chicago: University of Chicago Press, 1992), pp. 5–6.

5. Ibid.

6. Ibid.

7. James M. Buchanan, *Why I, Too, Am Not a Conservative: The Normative Vision of Classical Liberalism* (Northampton, MA: Edward Elgar Publishing, 2005).

8. Ibid. See also Robert Lawson, *James M. Buchanan, Why I, Too, Am Not a Conservative: The Normative Vision of Classical Liberalism*, Public Choice, Vol. 131 (2007), 249–251; D. Eric Schansberg, "*Why I, Too, Am Not a Conservative: The Normative Vision of Classical Liberalism*, [by] James M. Buchanan," *Journal of Markets and Morality*, Vol. 9, No. 2 (2006): 380–384; William A. Niskanen, *Reflections of a Political Economist:*

Selected Articles on Government Policies and Political Processes (Washington, DC: Cato Institute, 2008), 327–330.

9. James M. Buchanan, *Economics from the Outside In: Better Than Plowing and Beyond* (College Station: Texas A&M Press, 2001), pp. 148–150.

10. Ibid.

11. Buchanan, *Better than Plowing*.

12. Ibid., p. 21.

13. Vanderbilt University is a much more prestigious and expensive institution that the Methodist Episcopal Church South had founded in Nashville in the 1870s with generous contributions from financier Cornelius Vanderbilt (*http://www.vanderbilt.edu/about/history/*, retrieved August 14, 2012).

14. Interview with James M. Buchanan, December 1, 2006, Blacksburg, VA.

15. Ibid., p. 54.

16. Ibid., pp. 58–59, 64–65.

17. "The Worst Naval Disaster in U.S. History," *http://www.ussindianapolis.org*; Buchanan, *Better Than Plowing*, p. 65.

18. Buchanan's October 1987 lecture at Trinity University (*http://www.trinity.edu/nobel/*).

CHAPTER II.

THE BUCHANAN FAMILY IN NORTH AMERICA: FROM SCOTLAND TO TENNESSEE

James Buchanan's ancestors were among the first Europeans to permanently settle on the Cumberland River in 1780, helping to build and defend what became Nashville, Tennessee. Over the course of the next 225 years, Buchanan family members became yeomen farmers, entrepreneurs, politicians, and educators. The family produced a governor, John Price Buchanan, in the 19th century, a college president, James S. Buchanan, in the early part of the 20th century, and many other educators plus the Nobel laureate in the latter part of the 20th century. For Tennesseans and the world, the story of this family is inspiring due to its independent spirit and strength of character.

The Buchanan family and the Buchanan name originated in Scotland and, according to one source, specifically from the region around Sterling near Edinburgh. While the exact origin of the name is unknown, the likely root is Buchan, which "may be from the Gaelic boc, bocan, deer; a place abounding in deer."[1] An alternative origin for the name is "house of the canon."[2]

The Buchanan family crest, *Clarior Hinc Honos*, means "Brighter Hence the Honor." The Buchanan name is variously spelled as Buchanan, Bucanan, Bucanion, Bucanen, Bucanon, Buchannan, Buchannon, Buchannen, Buchanon, Buchanen, and Bohannon.[3]

Along with many others, the Buchanans came to North America from Scotland by way of Ireland. At the beginning of the 17th century, people from the borderlands of England and Scotland were induced to relocate to Ireland, principally the province of Ulster in the north of that island. Most of these migrating Scots were Presbyterians, who, like their Catholic Irish counterparts, had faced both religious persecution by Anglican landowners in Northern Ireland and economic hardship such as bad harvests and famine, the decline of the linen industry, restrictions on trade, and tariffs on Irish goods being shipped to England.[4] Initially, new arrivals from Ireland to North America were referred to simply as Irish. After the famines of the 1840s generated a new wave of Irish Catholics, that label was applied to this latter group. Consequently those transplanted from Scotland to Ireland and then to the Americas have become known as Scots-Irish, or more colloquially as Scotch-Irish. The Scots-Irish would become the largest ethnic group among the first settlers of Tennessee.[5]

One of the most popular destinations for many of those Scots-Irish immigrants was Philadelphia, Pennsylvania. As a result of the religiously tolerant environment created by the Pennsylvania charter of privileges in 1701, Philadelphia became an attractive location for the mainly Presbyterian immigrants from Ulster. More than a quarter of a million people left Northern Ireland before 1776, and another hundred thousand followed after 1783.[6]

As the population grew, Scots-Irish immigrants began to look beyond the crowded seaport to the western frontier. Eventually some moved from Philadelphia and other parts of Pennsylvania, traveling south into the valleys of the Blue Ridge Mountains in Virginia and the Carolina region in hopes of establishing a new life with abundant, fertile farmland, free from rent and tithe.[7]

Early lists of American immigrants include the following: a Jane Buchanan who came to New Jersey in 1664, an Alexander Buchanan who was banned to America in 1678, a John Buchanan who moved to Boston in 1751, and a David Buchanan who arrived there the next year.[8]

Colonial Virginia records report a John Buchanan having emigrated from Ireland to Virginia in the mid-1730s. This John Buchanan married Margaret Patton in 1749.[9] The records of the Virginia Regiment list a John Buchanan, almost certainly the man just mentioned, as "lieutenant of foot" in March 1742. He rose through the ranks to captain later in 1742 and to colonel by September 1744. Colonel John Buchanan died in 1769 in Botetourt County, Virginia. These early records refer to more than one John Buchanan, perhaps of different generations of related families.

By 1840, there were 445 Buchanan households in the United States, with the largest number living in Pennsylvania. Today there are 25,696 Buchanan households in the nation. Texas, with 2,085, has the largest number of such families, and Tennessee ranks fifth with 1,357.[10]

Lancaster County, Pennsylvania, was a magnet for many immigrants from Ireland, including a number of Buchanans. The earliest evidence of settlers from Ireland is the founding of Donegal Presbyterian Church of Lancaster County in 1719 or 1720 by settlers from County Donegal, Ireland, from which some Buchanan families emigrated.[11]

A James Buchanan died on March 4, 1746, leaving a last will and testament in the Lancaster County records, naming his son William an heir and a Walter Buchanan executor. Arthur Buchanan died in 1767, mentioning in his will his parents, Richard and Martha Buchanan, a brother, James Buchanan, and a sister, Janet Buchanan.[12] A total of five Buchanans filed a will in 18th-century Lancaster County, and another three are reported in the county's intestate records.[13] The Buchanan name was well established in the American colonies and in the region of Pennsylvania and Virginia by the middle of the 18th century. One of the challenges of this research is that so many Buchanans were living in the Atlantic Colonies by the mid-1700s, and almost every family included a John and a James.[14]

By the 1750s the John Buchanan who would eventually make his way to Tennessee lived in Lancaster County. A land transaction in 1766 locates a John Buchanan property in Lancaster County adjacent to the property of William Trindle.[15] This connection is important because in 1755 John Buchanan married Jane Trindle, the daughter of William. John Buchanan may have been born in Williamsburg, Virginia, or in Pennsylvania, or he may have emigrated from Ireland.[16]

Another Buchanan of Lancaster County is James Buchanan, the 15th president of the United States. President Buchanan's father immigrated to North America from County Donegal, Ireland, and then to Lancaster County in the 1780s.[17] That particular James Buchanan arrived

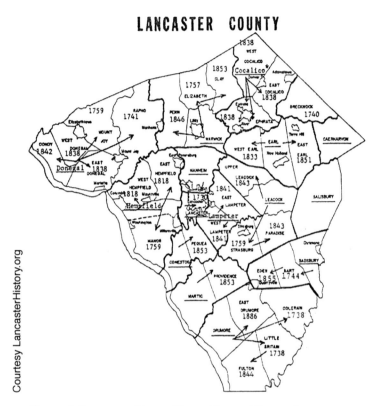

Figure 1. Lancaster County Townships and Boroughs

well after the John Buchanan family had departed from Pennsylvania, so any possible connection between the two Buchanan families would have been several generations before the birth of President Buchanan's grandfather.

A brief introduction to the Buchanan family followed in this book is warranted to avoid confusion over the names. The head of the family is John Buchanan, who will be iden-

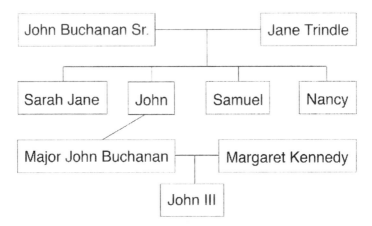

Figure 2. Family tree for first three Buchanan generations

tified as John Senior. He lived from sometime in the 1720s or 1730s to 1787, when he was killed by Indians in what would become Tennessee. His son John will be identified as Major John, a title earned in the Tennessee militia sometime in the 1780s or 1790s. He was born in 1759 in Pennsylvania and died in 1832 in Nashville, Tennessee. Major John's son John, who will be identified as John III, was born in 1787 in Nashville and died in 1834 in Williamson County, Tennessee.

The John Buchanan family of interest was among the many early settlers who moved, with or without official sanction, from Virginia and Pennsylvania to the frontier west of the Appalachian Mountains. One settler of the period described that migration:

That tract of country which lies between the Blue Ridge and the Alleghany mountains is, I think, less fertile than any part of Virginia. Near the Alleghany it is settled chiefly by the Scotch and Irish, who, on account of the cheapness of the land, have removed hither in prodigious shoals from the back part of Pennsylvania and Maryland.[18]

The evidence is not clear as to the route the Buchanans took on leaving Pennsylvania. Different writers have offered different versions. One historian records that the Buchanan family moved to North Carolina near Guilford Courthouse.[19] A North Carolina pay voucher indicates that a John Buchanan served in the North Carolina militia during the Revolutionary War. Moreover, the North Carolina legislature rewarded the Tennessee Buchanans with land grants.[20] Other writers suggest the family moved to Tennessee from South Carolina. South Carolina archives indicate that more than one John Buchanan served for some period in the state militia during the Revolutionary War.[21] A census of the early members of the Cumberland settlements in Tennessee states that the Buchanan family moved to the Watauga Settlements in what became upper East Tennessee before moving to Kentucky and eventually to the bend in the Cumberland River. However, if the Buchanan family stopped in the Watauga Settlements, that fact is not recorded in the materials concerning the settlements.[22]

We can state with certainty only that John Buchanan Senior and his family lived in Lancaster County, Pennsylvania, in the 1750s and arrived at the bend of the Cumberland River, where Nashville, Tennessee, would later be located in 1779.

Settlement of the Bend of the Cumberland

By the late 18th century, European explorers and frontiersmen had visited the area along the Cumberland River in today's Kentucky and Tennessee many times. Sometime after the mid-1700s, the French hunter and trader Timothe de Monbroen built a cabin near a natural salt lick frequented by buffalo and other animals at the bend of the Cumberland River, where the city of Nashville was later founded. That location became known initially as the French Lick. Pioneer Isaac Lindsey visited the area in 1769 along with several other explorers known as long hunters, so called because they made hunting trips that lasted for years.[23] Kasper Mansker, another of the most famous Cumberland pioneers, made an extended hunting expedition along the river in 1771–1772.[24] However, there were no permanent white settlers until the end of 1779.

The only viable overland route was by way of what is known as the Wilderness Road.[25] Almost certainly at least some of the Buchanan family followed this route on their way first to Kentucky and then to Tennessee. Beginning near the present-day border between North Carolina and Tennessee, the trail covered a rugged 200 miles across East Tennessee through the Cumberland Gap to the central Kentucky bluegrass settlement of Boonesborough (Figure 3).

The trip involved crossing five major rivers and many streams and walking and riding up and down steep slopes on a "road" no wider than a horse with a pack could navigate. In 1775, the Transylvania Company, headed by Richard Henderson, commissioned Daniel Boone to accommodate Indian rights and establish a route across the mountains

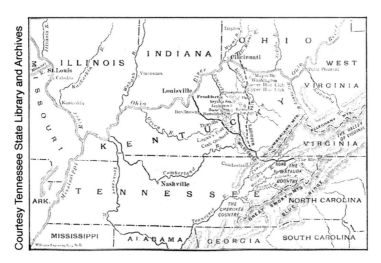

Figure 3. Wilderness Road

from the then-western settlements of Virginia to the Great Meadow of Kentucky. Boone and his party used existing natural paths and trails but hacked much of the trail from wilderness. Once the trail was initially marked, travelers designated the easternmost point on the road as the Block House for a fortified structure built in 1777 by Captain John Anderson. It is one mile north of the present North Carolina-Tennessee line in Washington County, Tennessee.

In December 1779, the first group that intended to settle permanently on the bend of the Cumberland arrived, led by James Robertson, a stalwart of Tennessee history. A second group headed by Robertson's co-leader, John Donelson, arrived early in 1780 after an arduous trip by river starting on the Holston in upper East Tennessee, then down the Tennessee River to its confluence with the Ohio River, and up the Cumberland to the bend.[26]

While the exact details are not clear, most accounts show the John Buchanan family splitting into two groups. One report documents the young (Major) John and at least one of his brothers traveling from what would become east Tennessee across the Cumberland Plateau to the French Lick, with or even before James Robertson's party.[27,] The rest of the family, led by John Buchanan Senior, came by horseback to the Cumberland from settlements in Kentucky. At the time, the trip from Kentucky south through the Cumberland Gap was considered the safer route.[28] In any case, John Buchanan Senior moved his wife, Jane, three sons—Alexander, (Major) John, and Samuel—and two daughters, Sarah Jane and Nancy, to the Cumberland River area in late 1779 and early 1780.[29]

Pioneers referred to the winter of 1779–1780 as the "Hard Winter." Surviving records tell of the travelers' difficulties. "The horses all died for cold & want of salt, but one." Hunger drove the stranded party to eat one of its dogs.[30] The condition of the trail itself was rough, and the weather conditions made a challenging journey even more difficult.

A Boston newspaper published a letter by a settler who described the trip along the road to the Kentucky settlements. On leaving the eastern terminus at Captain Anderson's Blockhouse, the traveler states:

> *The badness of the road from the block house is not easily described. From the rugged ascents and descents, which seemed absolutely impassable; and from the mire, which was every step up to my horses [sic] knees, occasioned by heavy rains, which had fallen a few days*

before, I had hard work to go a mile in an hour.[31]

For a family traveling with livestock, the trip could take 20 days or more, depending on the weather and conditions along the way. The Boston writer tells of his trip in the company of several hundred other settlers:

I believe no company ever had so disagreeable a time of it through the wilderness. Out of 22 days we had only 4 in which it did not rain and thunder most excessively.

We, however, all got safe through, notwithstanding many of the company, while sick, rode from morning 'till [sic] evening in the rain. We generally marched about ten miles in a day. Were [sic] never disturbed by the Indians, except once they fired on some of our company, who were out a hunting; but we frequently saw the effects of their cruelties. Scarce a day but we found the marks of a defeated company.[32]

The threat of Indian attack on frontier settlers was common during this time. Native Americans were responding to the increasing encroachment on and settlement of their hunting grounds, the trade abuses by settlers and land speculators, and the deliberate and repeated violations of treaties. Since many Native American Indians wanted to maintain their culture and protect their lands, they felt that white settlers needed to be eliminated.[33]

The challenges of the trip may have provided a foundation for the young John Buchanan's reputation as an Indian fighter and led to his eventual promotion to major in the militia. By one estimate, Indians killed an average of 100 travelers a year on the Wilderness Road, and over the course of the first two decades of settlement in Kentucky alone, 3,600 died in attacks.[34] In a letter written in 1780, another traveler on the road reported arriving safely in Kentucky:

> *Through an uninhabited Country the most rugged and dismal I have ever passed through, there being thousands of dead Horses & Cattle on the Road Side which occasioned a continual Stench; and one Half the way there were no Springs. . . . what made the Journey still more disagreeable was the continual apprehension we were under, of an Attack from the Indians, there not being one Day after we left Holston [Valley], but News was brought us of some Murders being committed by those Savages.*[35]

Those moving on from Kentucky to Tennessee endured still another difficult trek following the Cumberland River to its bend at the French Lick. Despite the hazards, the settlers arrived by the hundreds and soon by the thousands. On May 13, 1780, 256 white men signed a document known as the Cumberland Compact. The document created an early form of representative government by allocating representation of each of seven forts to a 12-man "Tribunal of Notables" that carried out governmental functions prior to the establishment of Davidson County three years later.[36] The group that signed the compact included a James Buchanan and his son, James Junior, but no members of the John Buchanan family signed.[37] James Buchanan may well have been related to John Senior, but the connection is unclear. Whether or not

James and John Senior were related, the form of the compact would interest the Nobel-winning James Buchanan of the 20th century because of his study of contracts and constitutions.

Based on the number of signers, we can estimate that by the spring of 1780 there were approximately 1,000 white settlers plus a number of slaves in the Cumberland region. Harriette Simpson Arnow ably chronicled the lives of the ordinary people who settled the Cumberland region in the 1780s and 1790s. Through meticulous combing of diaries, wills, inventories, and other public records, her books *Seedtime on the Cumberland* and *Flowering of the Cumberland* provide a remarkably complete picture of the lives and even the physical characteristics of the Cumberland settlers, including the Buchanan family. She described John Senior as "tall and spare, blue-eyed, black-headed."[38]

The first settlers of the Cumberland arrived in the winter of 1779-1780, when it was cold enough to freeze the Cumberland River and to allow people to walk across, or so historians have recorded.[39] However they arrived, some of the Buchanan men, almost certainly Major John and his brother Alexander, were reportedly at the bend of the Cumberland in late December 1779. They built a station on the south bank of the Cumberland on high ground above the river. This structure was first known as French Lick Station and later Fort Nashborough.[40] Shortly thereafter George Freeland built another station on the opposite side of Lick Branch.[41]

A station consisted of several cabins within a stockade with blockhouses at each corner. Today, a replica of Fort Nashborough commemorates the settlement in the bend of

Figure 4. Fort Nashborough

the Cumberland, but the replica is much smaller than the actual fort and not at the exact location of the original. Over the course of the intervening 230 years, the riverbank at the bend has changed. The first Fort Nashborough covered about two acres, an area large enough to accommodate a number of families.[42]

A Precarious Existence

Some leaders of the white settlers who moved into east Tennessee and later the Cumberland region attempted to reach peaceful agreement over land claims with the native Indian tribes living there, but fraudulent dealing as well as differences among those Indians resulted in frequent bloody clashes as whites tried to push the frontier westward. Consequently, even after running the gauntlet of the Wilderness Road, the new settlers had to remain constantly vigilant, as the area continued to be dangerous for them.

In late March 1781, the Buchanan brothers, Major John and Alexander, just managed to evade a party of Indians who were apparently organizing for an attack.[43] As it turned out a few days later, on April 2, a large force of Indians attacked Fort Nashborough in an affair known as the Battle of the Bluff.[44] The conflict began when reportedly the Indians taunted the settlers and lured a party of whites out of the station. The group included 23-year-old Alexander Buchanan, who was wounded along with three others early in the affair; all four died of their wounds. The 19 who left the station dismounted to fight, and in the commotion their horses bolted, leading the Indians to pursue the animals. At that point the women in the station released a pack of settlement dogs that attacked the Indians. In the confusion the survivors of the white party managed to return to the station. During that mêlée John Buchanan Senior saw an Indian clubbing Edward Swanson and left the station to rescue him. Buchanan fired at the Indian, and he and Swanson were able to escape to the fort.

In April and May of 1784, the North Carolina Assembly "established a town at the bluff, and named it Nashville, in memory of General [Francis] Nash."[45] Nash was a Revolutionary War general who commanded a brigade at the Battle of Germantown in New Jersey, where he received wounds from which he later died.[46] The group of 70 survivors of the Battle of the Bluff, including Major

John Buchanan, James Robertson, and James Mulherrin, the husband of Nancy Buchanan, from the initial Nashville settlement, were awarded land grants by the assembly. In addition, the assembly provided for the heirs of a group of 63 men, including Alexander Buchanan, who died defending the Cumberland settlements. Finally, the assembly identified a group of settlers not originally entitled to grants under an act of 1782 but who "remained in the country and helped to defend it." These included John Buchanan Senior, who received a grant of 640 acres.[47] By 1784 the family had begun building a new station about four miles east of Nashville on Mill Creek.[48]

Indians continued to imperil the lives and well-being of the pioneer Buchanan family for the first 15 years of their arrival in middle Tennessee. The names of both John Senior and Samuel Buchanan appear on the first tax list for Davidson County in 1787.[49] In that year Indians attacked Samuel while he was plowing. Twelve Indians pursued him, and when he jumped down a creek bank, "they overtook him and killed and scalped him."[50] Samuel was 27 years old. Indians also killed John Buchanan Senior before the new station was completed.[51] They reportedly killed and scalped him while he sat at his own table.[52] Jane Trindle Buchanan, present at the attack, was said to have suffered from the memory of that experience for the remainder of her life.[53] Between January and December 1787, Indians killed at least 33 people in Davidson and Sumner counties.[54]

The only surviving Buchanan son, (Major) John was now head of the family. He had been born in January 1759 when the family was still living in Pennsylvania.[55] He was a man of average height for his time. His portrait, which

Figure 5. Major John Buchanan portrait, Tennessee State Museum

hangs in the Tennessee State Museum in Nashville, shows a sturdy man with the penetrating gaze of a leader.[56] In 1786 at the age of 27, (Major) John married Margaret Kennedy, the daughter of John Kennedy, another prominent member of the Cumberland community.[57] She died the following year, May 15, 1787, after giving birth to a son, John, the third of the line of the Buchanan family this book traces. In 1791 Major John remarried, this time choosing Sarah Ridley.

Sarah, or Sally, Ridley Buchanan was the daughter of George Ridley and Elizabeth Weatherford. She was born in 1773, some say in the Watauga settlements, the earliest permanent settlements of what would become upper east Tennessee.[58]

When first settled, Tennessee was claimed by both Virginia and North Carolina, but in 1783 North Carolina established its claim by designating the Cumberland region as Davidson County.[59] In 1784 the state of North Carolina appointed John Sevier as brigadier general for the district of Washington. At the same time, the name Nashborough was changed to Nashville in Davidson County, Washington District. "The principal officers of the militia of Davidson County were: Anthony Bledsoe, colonel; Isaac Bledsoe, first major; Samuel Barton, second major; Kasper Mansker, George Freeland, John Buchanan, and James Ford, captains."[60] Later reports refer to John as a major, indicating that he subsequently rose in the ranks.[61]

Another Indian attack occurred on Sunday, September 30, 1792. A large force of Chickamaugas, consisting of a mixed group of Creeks, Cherokees, and Shawnees, moved from the south near present-day Chattanooga toward the Nashville settlements. While some of their leaders assured Governor William Blount they wished to establish peaceful relations with the white settlers, this force gathered with the intention of attacking Nashville. Under the leadership of John Watts, one of a number of mixed-race people living along this frontier and the man who organized this Indian attacking force, the Chickamaugas approached the Buchanan Station east of Nashville. The Indian leaders apparently disagreed among themselves about the best

Figure 6. Buchanan Station

tactics, but during the night of September 30, the force attacked Buchanan Station, catching the small group of settlers by surprise.

Noise created when the attackers roused the station cows alerted the settlers. Morris Shane was on guard duty that night and first discovered the attack and fired on the Indians.[62] Though the defenders included only 19 men, by good marksmanship and good fortune they beat off the attackers. The attacking Indian force has been reported as numbering anywhere from 200 to 900.[63] Whatever the true count, the attackers certainly outnumbered the defenders by more than 10 to one.

Given the small number of defenders, only a few could man each of the four corner blockhouses. Among those inside Buchanan Station were Mrs. Shane and Sarah, or Sally, Buchanan, the wife of Major John. They "sprang from their beds without taking time to dress and started molding bullets."[64] Sally reportedly helped the defenders by moving through the station and supplying them with shot and whiskey. Legend has it that Sally melted pewterware into rifle balls, and thus she became the heroine of the event.[65]

Early in the fight at Buchanan Station, several Indian leaders were killed, and John Watts was seriously wounded. Even though the battle raged for two hours, during the night the attacking Indians finally abandoned the fight and left the territory. Over the next two years, the settlers inflicted many casualties on the Chickamaugas until John Watts sued for peace in 1794, effectively ending the serious threat to the white settlers of the Cumberland region.[66]

The amazing Sally Buchanan gave birth to her first child, son George, only 11 days after the battle on October 11, 1792. Major John and Sally had 12 more children. Almost every other year from 1792 until 1818, Sally Buchanan gave birth. The children included George, Alexander, Elizabeth, Samuel, William, Jane Trindle, James, Moses, Sarah, Charles, Richard, Henry, and Nancy Mulherrin Buchanan.

(See Appendix B for more information on this family.) As her role in the Battle of Buchanan Station would indicate, Sally was definitely no shrinking violet. According to historian Harriet Simpson Arnow, Sally weighed more than 200 pounds and was able to lift two and a half bushels of corn.[67]

From the earliest years the Buchanans were respected members of the new community. John Buchanan Senior was a member of the first Grand Jury of Davidson County in 1784.[68] Major John Buchanan served on juries in civil cases and mixed with the most prominent settlers of the new territory.[69] Even though he did not serve in the Davidson County Court, the legislative branch of county government, his brother-in-law James Mulherrin served many terms.[70]

A fascinating document that survives from Major John is a manuscript known as Buchanan's *Arithmetic*. Bound in a hide cured from a deer that Major John himself killed, the book consists of definitions of arithmetic operations including addition, subtraction, multiplication, division, and square roots, with several examples of each neatly printed by hand. The book was certainly prepared by Major John for his own edification, and possibly for instructing others, perhaps his children. He was a man with the interest, initiative, and curiosity to prepare for more than a life of subsistence. It is a most remarkable document. The materials accompanying the *Arithmetic* include notes provided by a descendant of Major John that detail some history of the document. It now resides in the Tennessee State Library and Archives but is available for public inspection under close supervision. A digital copy may be seen in the Buchanan Family Reading Room of the James Walker Library at Middle Tennessee State University.

Figure 7. Major John Buchanan's Arithmetic

As noted earlier, the state of North Carolina issued land grants to (Major) John Buchanan, his brother Alexander's heirs, and their father, John Senior, with each receiving 640 acres in the Cumberland area.[71] Records of deeds in Davidson County and what in 1804 became Rutherford County indicate that Major John acted as a surveyor, just one of several ways by which he supplemented his income.[72] His name appears in that capacity in many deeds filed from 1788 until nearly 1800.[73] He surveyed at least two parcels that he acquired himself. By the time of his death, he owned land in Davidson, Williamson, Rutherford, and Wilson counties.[74]

THE PIONEER ECONOMY

Initially the pioneer settlement survived as a subsistence economy. A few cattle, hogs, chickens, horses, and mules plus a crop of corn, vegetables, and perhaps cotton were all the settlers could manage.[75] On their difficult trip into the Cumberland region, the settlers were able to bring only the farming tools they might carry themselves or on their packhorses. As a result, the first tools for planting and working the ground were limited to hoes and simple plows. For example, an inventory of Samuel Buchanan's property at the time of his death in 1787 included a simple plowpoint that could have been carried by a packhorse.[76] The paths traveled did not accommodate wagons until 1795.

Typically, the first crop to be planted was corn. After a cabin was built, some land became available for cultivating. Before the stumps were cleared, the planting would be done among the stumps. Then, following Indian fashion, the settler might plant beans, pumpkins, and squash between the rows of corn.[77] Families had to divert labor from crop production to provide security for the station during those early years. Even with diligence, many deaths, including that of Samuel Buchanan, occurred when settlers were attacked by Indians while tending their farms.[78]

Fairly quickly, however, the Cumberland pioneers moved beyond the subsistence level. Arnow argues the Buchanans and others were not "one horse farmers." They brought some home furnishings as well as farm implements on their journey from the east. Samuel Buchanan brought a fiddle, which suggests the family enjoyed some degree of culture.[79] The settlers were not just landowners but farmers, and working together with a few slaves they were able to create large, stump-free fields. By 1787 James Robertson already had two 15-acre fenced fields.[80] Within 10 years of arriving, middle Tennessee farmers were exporting some of their surpluses. They were selling corn, sometimes in the form of fattened hogs, pork, or whiskey. The new Buchanan Station eventually included one of the first gristmills in the area. Competition evidently followed quickly, for between 1793 and 1796 eight mills were built in Davidson County.[81]

Lacking the convenient transportation modes of today, pioneer farmers found that whiskey was an attractive vehicle for exporting their corn to outside markets. The U.S. Congress imposed an excise tax on distilled spirits in 1791, which inspired the so-called Whiskey Rebellion in western Pennsylvania, but Congress excluded the Southwest Territories, as Tennessee was known then, from the provisions of the law. As a result, Tennesseans were encouraged to export their whiskey to neighboring states at a cost advantage.[83] Not all the whiskey was exported, of course. The first tavern in Nashville was opened as early as 1784, and by the mid-1790s Nashville was home to several taverns and inns licensed to sell whiskey and other spirits. The operators even included an African-American, "a certain Negro called Bob," who was licensed to sell food and liquor.[84] Today middle Tennessee whiskey is still an important export product of the Jack Daniels distillery in Lynchburg and the George Dickel distillery in nearby Normandy.[85]

Despite the whiskey making, these early Tennesseans were "very strict observers of Sundays," according to French visitor Andre Michaux. Although most homeowners owned Bibles in those early years, the only established minister was Thomas B. Craighead of Nashville. There were no buildings yet in the Cumberland region exclusively devoted to worship.[86]

By the mid-1780s cotton was already an important crop in the new settlements. Arnow calls middle Tennessee the first "Cotton Kingdom" of the new United States.[87] By that time Cumberland settlers were selling cotton to buyers in Kentucky.[88] A report written in 1792 that area cotton crops were producing 800 pounds per acre notes that "the staple is long and fine."[89] After peace was achieved with the Indians, safe transport on the Tennessee River greatly improved the economic opportunities for early Tennesseans through trade between east and middle Tennessee and New Orleans and promoted further population growth. In 1792 a visitor to the Cumberland reported:

Wheat, barley, oats, rye, buckwheat, indian corn, pease

[sic], beans, potatoes, of both sorts, flax, hemp, tobacco, indigo, rice, and cotton, have already been planted in that settlement, and they all thrive in great perfection.[90]

Before the end of the 18th century, Nashville was already thriving, and although by that early date it was the established market center, other communities such as Murfreesboro had developed in the area.[91] Finally in 1795 a wagon road was opened between Knoxville and the Cumberland region, which aided the movement of cotton and other crops to a wider market.[92]

By 1804 there were 24 cotton gins in and around Nashville. Farmers shipped Cumberland-area cotton by river east to Pennsylvania.[93] An indication of the importance of the crop was the 1801 establishment by the state government of an inspection system to label cotton by quality.[94]

The end of the Indian threat and the sale of Chickasaw lands in west Tennessee in 1818 led to rapid development of the rich farmlands in the Mississippi River valley. Consequently by 1820 the opening of west Tennessee and other areas drove cotton prices down and eliminated cotton as the main cash crop for middle Tennessee.[95] At that point middle Tennessee farmers were compelled to diversify their crops.

During these first decades of Tennessee's history, the Buchanan family grew as it prospered. Ten of the 14 Buchanan children married, so the legacy of Major John and Sally was passed to an ever-larger family.[96]

The remarkable aspect of this story is how quickly the area was settled, from no permanent white settlers in 1779 to thousands within a dozen years. A census conducted in September 1791 of the area known as the Territory of the United States South of the River Ohio or Southwest Territory, which included the sections of Tennessee then settled, reported a total population of 35,691. Of that total, 7,042 lived in middle Tennessee, or the Mero District as it was then known.[97] One estimate is that by the end of the 18th century 100,000 settlers had crossed the Appalachians either by river or overland. When Tennessee joined the Union in 1796, its population was about 80,000. By the 1800 census Kentucky's population was 220,000 and Tennessee's 105,602.[98]

Along with trade and population growth came political development to accommodate the territory. On August 10, 1803, George Buchanan, perhaps a cousin of Major John, was one of more than 200 citizens primarily from the Stewart's Creek and Stones River areas of Davidson and Williamson counties who petitioned the state legislature to create a new county. Thus on October 27, 1803, the legislature approved the creation of Rutherford County in what is now the state's geographical center.[99] Until the creation of Bedford County in 1807, Rutherford County extended to the Alabama line. Rutherford County would later become the home of this story's Buchanan line, including Nobel laureate James Buchanan.

From 1804 to 1811, the county seat of Rutherford County was a community in the northwest corner known as Jefferson. By 1811, the population growth had shifted farther south and east toward the center of the county, and many citizens began to demand of the state legislature that the county seat be moved. Eventually some property near Stones River owned by William Lytle was chosen, and

Murfreesboro became the county seat.[100] Extended Buchanan family members, the McGills, moved to Rutherford County in 1819. James McGill Buchanan takes part of his name from that family.[101]

NOTES

1. Sherry Irvine, "Thinking about Scottish Surnames," http://www.last-names.net/Articles/Scottish-Names.asp.

2. Ancestry.com, *The Buchanan Name in History* (Provo, UT; The Generations Network, 2005), p. 12. A canon is a law, or body of rules, often associated with a religious body, according to *Webster's New World College Dictionary*, 4th ed. (New York: Macmillan U.S.A., 1999), p. 214.

3. Ibid.

4. Wayland F. Dunaway, *The Scotch-Irish of Colonial Pennsylvania* (Hamden, CT: Archon Books, 1962), pp. 29–31.

5. Wayne C. Moore, "Paths of Migration," in *First Families of Tennessee: A Register of Early Settlers and Their Present Day Descendants* (Knoxville, TN: East Tennessee Historical Society, 2000), p. 25.

6. R. J. Dickson, *Ulster Emigration to Colonial America, 1718–1775* (London: Routledge & Kegan Paul, 1966), pp. 222–223; and David Noel Doyle, *Ireland, Irishmen, and Revolutionary America, 1760–1820* (Dublin: Published for the Cultural Relations Committee of Ireland by Mercier Press, 1981), p. 51.

7. Dickson, pp. 224–226.

8. Source: "Buchanan Family Crest," http://www.4crests.com/buchanan-family-crest.html, retrieved December 17, 2008.

9. Source: "Patton Genealogy," http://lady3248.tripod.com/

pattongenealogypg4.htm, retrieved July 21, 2010.

10. *The Buchanan Name in History*, pp. 23, 59.

11. Retrieved December 14, 2010, from Donegal Presbyterian Church, *http://www.donegalpresbyterianchurch.org/index2.htm*.

12. Lancaster County, PA, Will Book I, 1–5; B-1–457.

13. Eleanore Jane Fulton and Barbara Kendig Mylin, *An Index to the Will Books and Intestate Records of Lancaster County, Pennsylvania 1729–1850* (Baltimore, MD: Genealogical Publishing, Co. Inc., 1974), pp. 6, 58.

14. Lloyd Dewitt Bockstruck, *Virginia's Colonial Soldiers* (Baltimore, MD: Genealogical Publishing, 1998); *The Complete George Washington Papers*, Library of Congress, *http://memory.loc.gov/ammem/gwhtml/gwhome.html*, retrieved September 26, 2007.

15. In Colonial Pennsylvania records for Cumberland County, PA, "Application for Land Warrants 1734–1865," there is an application dated August 22, 1766, from James Silver for land purchased from William Trindle joining land owned by John Buchanan in East Pennsborough. East Pennsborough and Cumberland County were originally part of Lancaster County. Retrieved September 11, 2007, from *http://ftp.rootsweb.com/pub/usgenweb/pa/1pa/land/1766land01.txt* and *http://www.ephistory.org/east_pennsboro.htm*.

16. Some genealogical records have John Buchanan born in Ramelton, County Donegal, Ireland, in 1727, others in Williamsburg, VA, in 1738.

17. Phillip Shriver Klein, *President James Buchanan: A Biography* (University Park, PA: Pennsylvania State University, 1962), pp. 1–3.

18. G. Herbert Smith, "A Letter from Kentucky," Mississippi Valley Historical Review, Vol. 19, No. 1 (June, 1932), p. 92.

19. Harriet Simpson Arnow, *Flowering of the Cumberland* (New York: Macmillan, 1963), p. 8.

20. *Treasurer's and Comptroller's Papers, Revolutionary War Pay Vouchers* (State of North Carolina, Department of Cultural Resources); *State Records of North Carolina*, Walter Clark, ed., Vol. XIX, 1782–1784, pp. 571–573. The North Carolina state archives report more than one John Buchanan as having served in the state militia during the Revolution.

21. Harriet Simpson Arnow, *Seedtime on the Cumberland* (New York: Macmillan, 1960), p. 206, n. 10. Samuel Cole Williams, *Tennessee During the Revolutionary War* (Knoxville, TN: University of Tennessee Press, 1974), p. 108. When the Buchanans reached the Cumberland, they were joined by the Mulherrin brothers, James, John, and William. According to Mulherrin family genealogies, the family lived in Ninety-Six, SC, before moving to Tennessee.

22. Richard Carlton Fulcher, *1780–1790 Census of the Cumberland Settlements: An Enumeration of the Inhabitants of Record in Davidson County, Being at Times in North Carolina, and the Territory South of the River Ohio* (Brentwood, TN, February 1, 1979).

23. Archibald Henderson, *The Conquest of the Old*

Southwest (Seattle, WA: The Wide World School, 2001). http://www.worldwideschool.org/library/books/lit/historical/TheConquestoftheOldSouthwest/legalese.html, retrieved August 27, 2007.

24. Walter Durham, "Kasper Mansker: Cumberland Frontier," *Tennessee Historical Quarterly*, Vol. XXX, No. 2 (Summer 1971), pp. 154–177. Mansker was the son of a German immigrant who arrived in Pennsylvania about 1749. Kasper was a stalwart among the Cumberland settlers and established his own station north of Nashville. A replica of Mansker's Station is located in Goodlettsville, TN, on the boundary of Davidson and Sumner counties.

25. Ellen Eslinger, *Running Mad for Kentucky* (Lexington, KY: University of Kentucky, 2004), p. 6.

26. Paul Bergeron et al., *Tennesseans and Their History* (Knoxville, TN: University of Tennessee Press, 1999), pp. 30–31. For more on the journey of James Robertson, see Katherine R. Barnes, "James Robertson's Journey to Nashville: Tracing the Route of Fall 1779," *Tennessee Historical Quarterly* 35 (Summer 1976), pp. 145–161.

27. Harriet Simpson Arnow, *Seedtime*, p. 232, has the Buchanans building a station near the French Lick before Christmas 1779.

28. The census of the early settlers mentioned above records a group of the family traveling with the Donelson party by river. However, there is no mention of the family in Donelson's journal.

29. Sarah Jane Buchanan married James Todd, and according to a Todd family history, the marriage took place in 1777 in

Lancaster, PA. James Todd then moved to Kentucky and on to Tennessee. That chronology is consistent with the reported history of the Buchanans and would indicate that James and Sarah Jane traveled with the Buchanans.

30. Eslinger, *Running Mad for Kentucky*, p. 35.

31. G. Herbert Smith, "A Letter from Kentucky," *Mississippi Valley Historical Review*, Vol. 19, No. 1 (June, 1932), p. 92. The letter was published in 1785.

32. Ibid., p. 95.

33. Ronald N. Satz, *Tennessee's Indian Peoples: From White Contact to Removal, 1540–1840* (Knoxville, TN: University of Tennessee Press, 1979), p. 68. For more on Tennessee's Native Americans, see John R. Finger, "Tennessee Indian History: Creativity and Power," *Tennessee Historical Quarterly* 54 (Winter 1995), pp. 286–305.

34. Eslinger, *Running Mad for Kentucky*, p. 50.

35. Ibid, pp. 38–39.

36. John R. Finger, *Tennessee Frontiers* (Bloomington, IN: Indiana University Press, 2001), p. 179. For more on the Cumberland Compact and early settlement, see A. W. Putnam, *History of Middle Tennessee or Life and Times of Gen. James Robertson* (Knoxville, TN: University of Tennessee Press, 1971). North Carolina named the county after William L. Davidson, who was an officer in the Revolutionary War.

37. The signers of the Cumberland Compact were essentially

the customers of land speculator Richard Henderson, and many of those buyers had come from the Watauga settlement of upper east Tennessee. There is no evidence that the John Buchanans were a part of that community, and they may have anticipated their eventual receipt of land grants from the state of North Carolina. The compact was an agreement to purchase land from Richard Henderson and Company and an elemental constitution providing for a governing body and electoral requirements. It turned out that Henderson's customers later had problems over their titles because North Carolina invalidated his claims to title for land in middle Tennessee. See John R. Finger, *Tennessee Frontiers* (Bloomington, IN: Indiana University Press, 2001), pp. 82, 106. Source: *http://books.google.com/books?id=u-0OMQw4N_sC&q=*. For further information, see *http://www.ajlambert.com/history/hst_cc.pdf*.

38. Arnow, *Flowering of the Cumberland*, pp. 7–8.

39. Robert E. Corlew, *Tennessee: A Short History*, 2nd ed. (Knoxville, TN: University of Tennessee Press, 1981), p. 52.

40. Arnow, *Seedtime on the Cumberland*, p. 232.

41. Arnow, *Flowering of the Cumberland*, p. 10.

42. *http://www.wnfoundersmuseum.org/ftnash.htm*, retrieved October 4, 2007.

43. John Haywood, *The Civil and Political History of the State of Tennessee* (Knoxville, TN: Tenase Co., 1823, 1969), pp. 118–120.

44. J. W. L. Matlock (ed.), "The Battle of the Bluffs: From the Journal of John Cotten," *Tennessee Historical Quarterly*, Vol.

XVII, No. 3 (Sept. 1959), p. 260. Matlock's source material has been questioned by Stanley J. Folmsbee, "The Journal of Joseph Cotton, the 'Reluctant Pioneer'—Evidence of Its Unreliability," *Tennessee Historical Quarterly*, Vol. 28, No. 1 (Spring 1969), pp. 84–94, but a similar description of the battle and the Buchanans' role is reported in Williams, *Tennessee During the Revolutionary War*, pp. 178–179.

45. Ibid., p. 204.

46. Corlew, *Tennessee: A Short History*, p. 53; General Francis Nash Chapter, Daughters of the American Revolution, *http://www.tndar.org/~francisnash/*, retrieved August 15, 2012.

47. Haywood, *The Civil and Political History of the State of Tennessee*, pp. 204–206. Note that those rewarded for having defended the territory do not include John Cotten.

48. Arnow, *Seedtime on the Cumberland*, p. 267. In 1785, an Archibald Buchanan moved to a 620-acre tract named Clover Bottom from Augusta County, Virginia. When Archibald died in 1806, the land was divided between his son James Buchanan and his uncle Robert Buchanan. James constructed a three-room log house in 1809, after which he married Lucinda "Lucy" East, with whom he had 16 children. Today volunteers from the Donelson-Hermitage Chapter of the Association for the Preservation of Tennessee Antiquities (APTA) manage this Buchanan Log House on 2910 Elm Hill Pike, Nashville. Kathy Lauder, adapted from the historical research of Nancy Helt and Joseph Wilson, "A History of the Buchanan Log House," *http://pages/prodigy.net/nhn.slate/nh0090.html*, retrieved December 16, 2008. Lauder notes that James Buchanan's tombstone (1841) reads: "Farewell my friends, as you pass by/ As you are now, so once was I/ As I am now, so

you must be / Prepare to die and follow me." His wife's (1865) followed: "As thou hast said, I follow you/ As all the rest must shortly do/ Then be not guilty of any crime/ So you may live in heaven sublime."

49. Corlew, *Tennessee: A Short History*, p. 55. http://www.geocities.com/Heartland/Plains/3661/TAX1787.html, retrieved August 15, 2012. "Davidson County was created in 1783 by an Act of the North Carolina legislature; named in honor of William Lee Davidson (ca. 1746–1781), colonial soldier, Revolutionary War officer in the North Carolina Third, Fourth and Fifth Regiments who was killed in action at the Battle of Cowans Ford on the Catawba River in North Carolina," http://www.rootsweb.com/~tndavids/nashgene.htm, retrieved August 15, 2012.

50. Arnow, *Seedtime on the Cumberland*, pp. 259–260, fn. 46. Haywood, *The Civil and Political History of the State of Tennessee*, p. 228.

51. Ibid., pp. 349, 356. One reason that Arnow is able to report on the possessions and activities of the Buchanan family is that they were recorded in the will and property inventories recorded when members of the family died or were killed. In the October 4, 1787, session of the Davidson Court, John Buchanan and James Mulherin took the "Oath of Administration" to serve as the administrators of the estate of John Buchanan Senior. *Records of Davidson Court*, Vol. C., p. 194.

52. Richard C. Fulcher, *1780–1790 Census of the Cumberland Settlements* (Brentwood, TN: Richard Carlton Fulcher, Genealogist, 1979), p. 12.

53. Helen Hartman Brandon, *Hartman-Buchanan Family*,

October 1988, Tennessee State Library and Archives, p. 74.

54. Haywood, pp. 229–230.

55. See the family genealogy in Appendix B.

56. Arnow, *Flowering of the Cumberland*, p. 85, states that Major John Buchanan was "a thick set man, five feet, six or eight inches tall."

57. Davidson County, TN, Wills Book 1784-181 (Tennessee State Library and Archives).

58. See Arnow, *Flowering of the Cumberland*. Davidson County, TN, Wills Book 1784–1816, Tennessee State Library and Archives microfilm reel #427. Here again, there is no documentation to substantiate Sarah Ridley's birth at Watauga.

59. *Tennessee Encyclopedia of History and Culture, http://tennesseeencyclopedia.net/entry.php?rec=356*, retrieved August 15, 2012.

60. Williams, *Tennessee During the Revolutionary War*, p. 254.

61. A. W. Putnam, *History of Middle Tennessee: Or Life and Times of General James Robertson* (Knoxville, TN: University of Tennessee Press, 1971). March 5, 1783, John Buchanan was appointed second lieutenant, pp. 186–718; January 6, 1784, John Buchanan took the oath as third captain, pp. 211–213. In Wells, *Davidson County Court Minutes* on October 4, 1787, there is a reference to Major John Buchanan, p. 88 (p. 274 in original).

62. Jeannette Tillotson Acklen, *Bible Records and Marriage*

Bonds (Nashville, TN: Clearfield Co., 1933, reprinted by Genealogical Publishing Co., 1995), pp. 130–131. This story is recorded in the Shane family Bible (Williamson County Archives).

63. Walter T. Durham, *Before Tennessee: The Southwest Territory 1790–1796* (Piney Flats, TN: Rocky Mount Historical Association, 1990), pp. 83–84, states that the Indians included 500 Creek, 197 Cherokee, and 30 Shawnee. His version of the story differs somewhat from others. For a version from the Native Americans' perspective, see *http://www.chickamauga-cherokee.com/buchanansstation.html*, retrieved August 15, 2012.

64. Acklen, *Bible Records*, pp. 130–131.

65. James A. Crutchfield, *Yesteryear in Nashville: An Almanac of Nashville History* (S.l. : s.n., 1981), p. 25; Arnow, *Flowering of the Cumberland*, pp. 25–29.

66. This story is pieced together from Haywood, pp. 356–359; Appleton's Encyclopedia, *http://famousamericans.net/sarahbuchanan/*, retrieved February 16, 2007; and Rolater, *Tennessee Encyclopedia of History and Culture*, *http://tennesseeencyclopedia.net/entry.php?rec=244*, retrieved August 15, 2012.

67. Arnow, *Flowering of the Cumberland*, p. 2.

68. Carol Wells, *Davidson County Court Minutes, 1783–1792* (Bowie, MD: Heritage Books, Inc. 1990), p. 1 (p. 4 in the original).

69. *Records of Davidson Court*, Vol. C, pp. 141, 146. In a civil suit in which he was the plaintiff, Buchanan was represented by Andrew Jackson. *Records of Davidson Court*, Vol. B, p. 153

(Tennessee State Library and Archives).

70. *Records of Davidson Court,* Vol. C, pp. 94, 155, 165, 199, 201 (Tennessee State Library and Archives).

71. *Records of the State of North Carolina,* Vol. XXIX, pp. 571–573.

72. Ibid., pp. 9, 18. In a parcel the he surveyed himself in 1786, he obtained 200 acres about four miles from Buchanan Station. In the same year he obtained another 640 acres.

73. E. K. Johns, *Deed Abstracts on Stones River from Deed Books A, B, C, D, E, F of Davidson County, Tennessee, 1784–1806* (Murfreesboro, TN: Rutherford County Historical Society, 1981), pp. 2–106.

74. Brandon, *Hartman-Buchanan Family,* p. 10, references Bessie Lee Batey Haynes, *History of Blackman Community* (November 1976).

75. Finger, p. 83.

76. Arnow, *Seedtime on the Cumberland,* p. 259.

77. Donald L. Winters, *Tennessee Farming, Tennessee Farmers* (Knoxville, TN: University of Tennessee Press, 1994), pp. 20–21.

78. Harriette S. Arnow, "The Pioneer Farmer and His Crops in the Cumberland Region," *Tennessee Historical Quarterly,* Vol. XIX, No. 4 (December 1960), p. 297.

79. Arnow, *Seedtime on the Cumberland,* p. 365. On Samuel's

death, a David Buchanan bought the fiddle for seven dollars.

80. Ibid., p. 296.

81. Durham, *Before Tennessee*, p. 231.

82. *History of Homes and Gardens of Tennessee, 1936* (Garden Study Club Of Nashville Collection), Tennessee State Library and Archives, Accession Number: 95-062, Date Completed: October 4, 1995, Location: I-E-7, Stack #2 and the Map Cases.

83. Finger, *Tennessee Frontiers*, p. 181.

84. Durham, *Before Tennessee*, pp. 228, 232–233.

85. For more on the distilleries in Tennessee, see Jeanne R. Bigger, "Jack Daniel Distillery and Lynchburg: A Visit to Moore County, Tennessee," *Tennessee Historical Quarterly* 31 (Spring 1972), pp. 3–21; Kay Baker Gaston, "George Dickel Tennessee Sour Mash Whiskey: The Story Behind the Label," *Tennessee Historical Quarterly* 57 (1998), pp. 150–167.

86. Arnow, *Seedtime on the Cumberland*, p. 15.

87. Arnow, *Seedtime on the Cumberland*, p. 298.

88. Winters, *Tennessee Farming*, p. 54.

89. Ibid., p. 54.

90. Ibid., p. 26.

91. Ibid., pp. 26–28. Murfreesboro, originally called Cannons-

burgh, was settled more than 20 years before it was chartered in 1811.

92. Durham, *Before Tennessee*, pp. 234–237.

93. Winters, *Tennessee Farming*, p. 54.

94. Ibid., p. 55. After farmers complained that the system depressed the price of lower-grade cotton, the legislature repealed the provisions on grading and labeling and abolished the entire inspection system in 1838.

95. Ibid, p. 28.

96. The last of that generation died in 1898. See family genealogy in Appendix B.

97. Walter T. Durham, *Before Tennessee: The Southwest Territory 1790–1796* (Piney Flats, TN: Rocky Mount Historical Association, 1990), p. 53.

98. Eslinger, *Running Mad for Kentucky*, pp. x, 210, 50; Finger, *Tennessee Frontiers*, p. 210.

99. Mabel Pittard, *Rutherford County* (Memphis, TN: Memphis State University Press, 1984), pp. 22–23, 131.

100. Terry Weeks, *Heart of Tennessee: The Story & Images of Historic Rutherford County* (Murfreesboro, TN: Courier Printing Co., 1992), pp. 26, 30.

101. Between 1796 and 1812, except for a one-day interlude in 1807 in Kingston, the state capital was located in Knoxville.

Then in 1812 it was moved to Nashville for five years and returned to Knoxville for one year in 1817. In 1818 the capital was again moved to Murfreesboro in Rutherford County, where it stayed until 1826, when it returned to Nashville permanently. *Tennessee Encyclopedia of History and Culture, http://tennesseeencyclopedia.net/imagegallery.php?EntryID= C028*, retrieved August 31, 2010.

CHAPTER III.

THE SECOND GENERATION: BUCHANANS OF THE 19TH CENTURY

A BURGEONING YOUNG TENNESSEE

By the time the Buchanan family had been in the Cumberland region for 20 years, the territory and the Union had changed dramatically. The United States had expanded beyond the original 13 states: Vermont became a state in 1791, Kentucky joined the Union in 1792, and Tennessee followed in 1796. Within the new state, the Tennessee legislature carved Williamson County out of Davidson County in 1799. Named after Dr. Hugh Williamson, a North Carolina statesman who had attended the U.S. Constitutional Convention of 1787, the county was bounded on the north and west by Robertson County and on the south by Indian Territory.[1]

The first tax records for the new political entity of Williamson County identify Major John Buchanan as an important landowner and taxpayer. The 1800 tax rolls indicate that he owned 2,840 acres in various tracts. He also paid the poll tax in Williamson County. In 1801 the name

John Buchanan Jr. appears in those records. Since John Buchanan Senior was killed in 1787, this John was likely the son of Major John, even though John III would be only 14 years old by this time. Thus, John III established himself with the help of his father in Williamson County at an early age. Other Buchanan names appear in the first tax book for the county until 1807, after which only the name John Buchanan appears through the end of that record in 1813. The tax records suggest that John III farmed a 200-acre tract along the Harpeth River and that the Buchanan family, including both Major John and other members of the extended family, owned another 1,820-plus acres in the county over the period 1801 through 1813.[2]

Major John and Sally appear in the 1820 census in Davidson County with 10 additional members of their household. They appear for the last time in the 1830 census, still in Nashville and living with four of their children. Sally died in 1831 at age 58 and Major John in 1832 at nearly 74. They are buried in a family cemetery on the site of the Buchanan Station property, where their graves with headstone are still intact and readable.

The next generation wasted no time in making a life and prospering. John Buchanan III married Margaret Sample on September 19, 1805, when he was 18 and she was 14.[3] They had 10 children between 1806 and 1823. The 1820 U.S. census records 33-year-old John Buchanan III, his wife, and eight children living in Williamson County. John III was already thriving by that time. The census reports that John's household in addition to his family included 16 slaves, nine males and seven females. The children included John Sample (1806), Peggy Ann (1807), William M. (1809),

Samuel (1810), Sarah (1812), Elizabeth (1815), Robert S. (1818), Mary B. (1820), and Thomas Buchanan (1823).[4] All of the children married except Samuel, who died in 1825, and all but Sarah had children; altogether this generation produced 58 offspring. The Buchanan family that began with John Senior and his five children had multiplied through generations in Tennessee, growing along with the state and the Cumberland community. By 1820, the population of Williamson County had reached 20,640—whites, free persons of color, and slaves.[5]

THE BUCHANAN FARM IN WILLIAMSON COUNTY

The size of the Buchanan farm and the presence of slaves indicate the family did more than simply provide for immediate needs. A history of Tennessee farming analyzes the relationship among farm size, number of slaves owned, and production of a subsistence corn crop.[6] The larger the farm or the number of slaves, the less acreage proportionately was devoted to corn. The composition of the Buchanan household and its assets suggest the family was able to devote more of its resources to producing for commercial purposes.

Though the country prospered and commercial farming was important, farm families of 19th-century middle Tennessee were, to the extent possible, self-sufficient. With few exceptions they grew their own food and made their own clothes. French visitor François André Michaux observed, "I am persuaded that not one in ten of them [farmers] are in possession of a single dollar, still each enjoys himself at home with the produce of his estate."[7] A shortage of hard money was always a problem in the farming community and especially so in the earliest days of Tennessee.

Corn remained the staple crop. It provided fresh roasting ears in the early season and cornmeal for cornbread, grits, mush, and other dishes the rest of the year. Settlers also continued to turn corn into whiskey. Farmers grew other grains such as wheat, oats, and rye, but these crops were less common. As a result, wheat flour for white bread was a luxury not often enjoyed. In the 1830s, records show the Buchanan family raised cotton, corn, wheat, and oats as well as hay and fodder for their livestock.[8]

Kitchen gardens supplied families with fresh vegetables during the summer months and into the fall. Those same vegetables might be dried or after 1840 canned for use during the rest of the year. Root cellars kept potatoes, carrots, turnips, and apples cool and available for longer periods as well. Trees and arbors provided apples, peaches, plums, cherries, grapes, and other fruits. Wild blackberries, plums, grapes, and other wild foods contributed to the family diet.[9]

Meat for the family table was also largely from home production. The Buchanan family raised cattle, sheep, and hogs along with geese and chickens.[10] As elsewhere in the South, the most common table fare was pork, followed by chicken. Fall hog killing, then as now, was a farm tradition. When temperatures dropped in the late fall, hogs were slaughtered to provide hams, sausage, bacon, and lard for the year. Some fresh pork was available after the hog killing, but most was salted and smoked, preserved for use later in the year. The Buchanan farm included a smokehouse.[11]

Beef was less widely available. Even though farm families kept cows for milk, butter, and cheese, beef was more difficult to preserve than pork. Consequently, when they ate beef, it was usually fresh. Chickens, turkeys, ducks, and geese were raised for both eggs and meat. Game such as deer, rabbits, and squirrels along with fish from area streams and rivers were other sources of table fare. Families had to purchase or barter for those foods not grown locally. Most notably, coffee, tea, and possibly refined cane sugar were bought "in town."[12]

In similar fashion, providing clothes for family members was largely a home enterprise. Farm families made most of their own clothes. A farm wife from neighboring Cheatham County recorded in her diary that she did everything from preparing the raw fibers to sewing the finished article of clothing. "I'm up & at the loom early & by dint of hard work get my cloth out."[13] Margaret Buchanan had a spinning machine and loom, so she and her household made their own cloth and probably also made clothes from that material.[14] By mid-century there were specialists in spinning and weaving, some on a share basis or for cash or barter. Most customers were still buying cloth to take home for sewing their own garments.

Farm families also met many of their other needs such as housing, outbuildings, and furniture; some even made shoes. Today we often speak of the past as a simpler time; in fact the Tennessee of the early 19th century and even later was anything but simple. The farm families of this era worked hard every day simply to provide their own food and shelter. They required skills and knowledge: when and what to plant, how to cultivate, when to harvest, how to preserve food, how to convert raw fiber into cloth, how to sew their own clothes, how to make the tools they needed, and many other aspects of living that few people today could match. It is fair to say that if John Buchanan of the 1820s were transported to the 21st century he would soon understand how to go to the modern supermarket and even how to manage the electric and electronic appliances on which we rely. However, a 21st century Tennessean of comparable age transported to the Tennessee of the 1820s would have difficulty even surviving. Was it a simpler time? Different, but hardly simpler!

In order to buy or barter for those foods and other goods the family could not produce, some production for commerce was necessary. In the 1790s the merchants operating in east and west Tennessee, where west refers to what today would be middle Tennessee, offered to sell for cash or to trade goods, mainly for furs or cotton. Through the early 19th century, store owners continued to be willing to accept farm products in exchange for their goods. Again, French observer André Michaux notes that barter usually worked to the advantage of the merchant. "These tradesmen . . . do not always pay in cash for the cotton they purchase but make the cultivators take goods in exchange, which adds considerably to their profit."[15] However, a cash economy was developing along with the increase in economic activity. Both farmers and merchants looked to trade in cash when possible.

Middle Tennessee farmers continued to rely on cotton as a cash crop into the middle of the 1800s, although other areas in the state and region became the dominant producers. Tobacco became an important cash crop early in the settlement of northern middle Tennessee. Even into the 21st century, that area remains the only part of the mid-state where tobacco is an important crop. Livestock was another key source of income for middle Tennessee. Pork production was particularly important. The extended Buchanan family raised hogs in Rutherford County through the war years of the 1860s. Middle Tennessee farmers were selling cattle and poultry, and Tennessee horses and mules were renowned throughout the South.[16] By the end of the century, a Buchanan farm would specialize in livestock.

In his will, prepared in January 1834, John Buchanan III bequeathed several hundreds of acres of land to his wife, Margaret, and their children. Each received large tracts of land plus slaves. Additionally, Margaret was to receive the household furnishings and farming equipment plus stock, including horses and oxen along with the animals raised to provide food. Together with equipment for the smokehouse, Margaret also received the spinning machine and loom. The properties left to others in the family included a blacksmith shop.[17] This family was clearly more than self-sufficient. By the time of John III's death, his children were already prepared to carry on the traditions established by their father and grandfather.

John Buchanan III died on June 29, 1834, at the age of 47 in Williamson County and was buried in a Buchanan family cemetery on the family farm. His headstone still stands, readable in the cemetery located in a modern, landscaped office park just north and east of Franklin adjacent to the present day U.S. Interstate 65.[18] This office park is near the huge Cool Springs Galleria shopping center and adjacent to the Nissan North America headquarters. The

Figure 8. Buchanan family cemetery in Cool Springs, Tennessee

value of the Buchanan farm site in the 21st century would be many millions of dollars.

Margaret Buchanan, John's widow, appears in the 1840 census living with two young males, almost certainly her sons Robert, 22, and Thomas, 17.[19] That census indicates the family was still farming but certainly on a considerably smaller scale. They owned three slaves, only one of whom was old enough to provide much help on the farm. The youngest son, Thomas, attended the Harpeth Male Academy in Franklin.[20] Margaret appears in 1850 and 1860 census records living with Thomas and his family.

Thus, by the mid-1800s after 70 years in residence, the Buchanans were established as prosperous and substantial members of the middle Tennessee community. War would change that condition for the family as it did for most of the American South.

Notes

1. *Acts of Tennessee 1799*, Chapter 3, *http://tennessee.gov/tsla/history/county/actwilliamson.htm*, retrieved January 19, 2009.

2. Louise Gillespie Lynch, *Tax Book I: Williamson County, Tennessee, 1800–1813* (Franklin, TN, 1971), pp. 2, 11, 12, 23, 24, 37, 38, 53, 54, 55, 75, 76, 98, 99, 126, 127, 128, 168, 201, 235, 265, 266, 297, 330.

3. Family history, *One World Tree*, Provo, Utah; 1820 U.S. Census, Williamson County, Tennessee, p. 15.

4. Thomas Buchanan, 1898. Davidson County, TN—Biographies—Buchanan Family. "History of the Buchanan Family," *http://files.usgwarchives.org/tn/davidson/bios/bchnan01.txt*, retrieved August 15, 2012. If the family had 10 children, one is obviously missing from the list, possibly one who died in childhood.

5. A handwritten notation in the beginning of the 1820 U.S. Census for Williamson County, TN.

6. Donald L. Winters, *Tennessee Farming, Tennessee Farmers* (Knoxville, TN: University of Tennessee Press, 1994), pp. 37–47.

7. Winters, *Tennessee Farming*, p. 30.

8. John Buchanan's *Last Will and Testament* (Williamson County, TN, Archives).

9. Winters, *Tennessee Farming*, pp. 30–32.

10. John Buchanan's *Last Will and Testament* (Williamson County, TN, Archives).

11. Ibid.

12. Winters, *Tennessee Farming*, pp. 32–34.

13. Ibid., p. 35.

14. Ibid., pp. 35–36.

15. Winters, *Tennessee Farming*, p. 49.

16. Ibid. pp. 53–67.

17. John Buchanan's *Last Will and Testament* (Williamson County, TN, Archives).

18. The address is 8 Corporate Centre, Caruthers Parkway, Franklin, TN. The cemetery is inside a rock wall on the neatly landscaped campus of the office building. As a result it should be protected for the foreseeable future.

19. Prior to the 1850 U.S. census, the name of only the head of the household was recorded. Beginning with the 1850 census, the name of every member of the household was listed.

20. Obituary of Thomas Buchanan, *Review Appeal*, Vol. XCVI, No. 221 (November 12, 1908).

CHAPTER IV.

Buchanans and the Civil War

The Fourth-Generation Buchanan Family in Tennessee

Thomas Buchanan married Rebecca Jane Shannon on November 5, 1846. Thomas first appears as head of a household in the 1850 census for Williamson County, identifying himself as a farmer with land valued at $4,500. Thomas and Rebecca would have five children: John Price, Mary Margaret, Susan Ann, Jennie Thomas, and James Shannon Buchanan.[1] In time John Price Buchanan became governor of Tennessee, James Shannon Buchanan became president of the University of Oklahoma, and daughter Jennie became a college teacher.

According to the censuses of 1860, 1870, and 1880, Thomas continued to live and farm in Williamson County. In the 1860 census he appears as a highly successful farmer with real estate valued at $16,000. The value of the typical middle Tennessee farm operated by its owner during the period 1850 to 1860 was slightly greater than $1,580. With real estate valued at $16,000, Thomas likely owned more than 1,000 acres, based on an average price of $13 per acre.² He also reported in the 1860 census personal property valued at $15,000, accounted for by the 22 slaves he owned. Those slaves included 14 females and eight males, but only nine of the slaves were in the prime working-age range of 14 to 60, two were 70 or more, and 11 were under 14.³ With the aid of slaves, Thomas probably raised cotton along with other crops on his substantial farm but still did not operate what could be called a plantation. The difference between a large farm and a plantation was whether the owner was a working owner who farmed alongside his workers or simply an owner who hired a professional manager. In any case Thomas Buchanan was wealthy relative to most of his neighbors but not an aristocrat.

In that period it was discovered that silkworms would thrive by feeding on mulberry leaves. In 1841, editors of the *Agriculturist* found a number of Williamson County farmers owning up to a million silkworms each. The Buchanan family may have been tempted to experiment with silk production in the 1830s and 1840s. Silk producers in Tennessee accounted for a thousand pounds of silk cocoons by 1840 and two thousand in 1850, with the result that Tennessee was the largest silk producer in the United States. Unfortunately, in the 1850s an unknown disease attacked the silkworms, and production plummeted. By 1860 silk production had largely disappeared from the state.⁴

During the decade of the 1840s, the Buchanan family benefited from the introduction of the railroad to middle Tennessee.⁵ In 1845 the state legislature provided incorporation and some aid to the establishment of the Nashville and Chattanooga Railroad. Construction did not actually begin until 1849, and the line was not complete to Chattanooga until 1854.[6] The development of the line from Nashville to Chattanooga passed through Murfreesboro, where the extended Buchanan family—actually the McGill family, into which John Price Buchanan would marry—lived. In fact, the location of the railroad played a major role in determining which communities became towns and which remained only villages. Buchanan farms in Williamson County were not the major beneficiaries of this first railroad since their property was west of the rail line, but the arrival of the railroad impacted land prices significantly. Thus, Buchanan family farmland likely increased in value as a result.

By 1860 three rail lines connected Nashville and Decatur, Alabama, on the Tennessee River. The first leg, owned by the Tennessee & Alabama Railroad, from Nashville to Mount Pleasant, Tennessee, passed through the cities of Franklin and Columbia. Connecting legs were owned by the Central Southern Railroad, linking Columbia and the Alabama state line, and the Tennessee & Alabama Central Railroad, operating the relatively short distance from the end of the Central Southern line on the state boundary to Decatur, Alabama. This railroad would have helped Thomas Buchanan significantly had it not been for the Civil War.

However, the Civil War intervened, and it was not until 1866 that the three operations merged and became the Nashville & Decatur Railroad. After the war, in 1872, this company was acquired by the Louisville & Nashville Railroad along with other lines to complete a system from Louisville to Birmingham and Montgomery, with access to the Gulf coast ports of New Orleans, Mobile, and Pensacola.[7]

The result was the opening of new markets for middle Tennessee farmers but also exposure to new competition.

The Civil War Years

During the war years of 1861 to 1865, Thomas Buchanan of Williamson County was in his late 30s and early 40s. Although his son John Price served in the war, there is no record that Thomas served.[8] By March 1862 the Union Army occupied most of Williamson and Rutherford counties. Thomas, whose children were still young, may have felt obligated to remain at home to protect his family and property.

Seven Southern states, South Carolina, Alabama, Georgia, Florida, Mississippi, Louisiana, and Texas, had already seceded from the Union before Tennessee joined the Confederacy.[9] After South Carolina military forces attacked the federal garrison at Fort Sumter near Charleston, the federal government requested the Upper South's assistance with the outbreak of war. The Upper South, including Tennessee, faced a horrendous choice: either to fight against the Lower South or to fight against the Union. Eventually, Tennesseans reversed their position and voted for secession, despite considerable opposition to secession in the eastern portion of the state. In addition to Tennessee, other Upper South states including Virginia, Arkansas, and North Carolina joined the Confederacy.[10]

By the fall of 1861, middle Tennessee had already felt the impact of war. In a letter dated October 24, 1861, a Franklin, Tennessee, native was appointed as an agent for the Confederate Army with authorization to impress food, wagons, animals, and slaves not willingly sold.[11] "Farmers close to Nashville complained loudly about pilfering of hogs, chickens, and timber by poorly provisioned and worse disciplined Confederate soldiers camped nearby, who acted 'with violence and utter contempt for *the rights of the sufferers.*'"[12] These events would have affected Thomas Buchanan and his family. Still, the farms of the area operated with some degree of continuity through 1861. Another letter written in December 1861 reports that in Williamson County "the neighborhood is generally healthy, the crops good and everything high [in price]."[13]

Confederate reverses in early 1862 with defeats at Mill Springs, Kentucky, and Forts Henry and Donelson in Tennessee resulted in the retreat of the Confederate forces south of Murfreesboro. From that point Federal troops periodically took whatever they chose from the local population. In September 1862, a Williamson County farmer recorded in his diary that with the combination of drought and war he was "not making more than half a crop."[14]

Conditions were even worse by the following spring. Passing through Bedford and Rutherford counties, a Confederate soldier observed, "The country wears the most desolate appearance that I have ever seen anywhere. There is not a stalk of corn or blade of wheat growing."[15] Around the same time, a Williamson County farmer noted in his diary:

> *The Federal soldiers have taken every horse and mule that I have. . . . They have broken into my smoke house repetedly [sic] and have taken all my hams. They have*

taken a goodeal [sic] of my corn and all of my hay and near all my fodder. My health is very bad. I will certenly [sic] go crazy.[16]

In addition to the confiscation of property and sustenance by the occupiers, local inhabitants were harassed by criminals.

The most striking manifestation of the fracturing of Middle Tennessee society was the proliferation of crime. During the latter part of the war, the region was engulfed by an indigenous crime wave of tidal proportions, a deluge of villainies committed by [Middle Tennesseans] against [Middle Tennesseans], which left no high ground for refuge. . . . A group of Rutherford County residents described their land that year [1864] as one 'where crime of every grade unrebuked, runs riot at noonday, where there is neither safety for the person or protection for the property of the citizen.'[17]

As a result, farmers were reluctant to plant, fearing the product of their efforts would be stolen.

For those in Williamson County, an even worse situation occurred when in November and December 1864, Confederate General John Bell Hood led the Army of Tennessee in an invasion of middle Tennessee. The Confederates suffered 7,500 casualties in the Battle of Franklin, and that was followed by the ultimate defeat of the western rebel forces in the Battle of Nashville. Over a five-week period from late November through

Christmas of 1864, almost 20,000 Confederates were killed, captured, wounded, or missing in action.[18] *Buchanan property, probably even the home place, was located just north of Franklin not far from the main road to Nashville. It is highly likely that the farm was damaged during the troop movements from Franklin to Nashville.*

Despite the obstacles imposed by the war, the exporting of cotton continued, even some from middle Tennessee. In 1864 a private shipping company in middle Tennessee shipped 500 bales via the Nashville and Chattanooga Railroad to Wilmington, North Carolina, where blockade runners managed to get it to Liverpool, England. The cotton was bought in Tennessee at 65 cents per pound and sold in England at two dollars.[19]

Near the formal end of hostilities in the spring of 1865, a Williamson County farmer and minister returning from the fighting in North Carolina reported a land devastated by war and stripped of livestock. He had so much to do in order to restore his farm to working order that he was unable to resume his circuit-riding ministry.[20]

Even though Thomas Buchanan may not have been directly involved in the war, his community was heavily impacted. His family circumstances were substantially reduced, and if the family was not impoverished, almost certainly the farm and properties were damaged.

The Young John Price Buchanan

Thomas and Rebecca Jane Buchanan's oldest child, John Price, was born on October 24, 1847.[21] Like his father, he was educated in the community schools of Williamson County and also received some private instruction. His father planned for him to attend college, as his younger siblings later would, but the Civil War interrupted those plans.[22]

Living in the maelstrom of war as a teenager, John Price Buchanan was inspired to leave home in 1864, when he was only 16 years old, to enlist in the Fourth Alabama Cavalry, Roddy's Escort. He reported in his "Soldier's Application for Pension" that while he was never in a major battle, he participated in "many skirmishes."[23] His unit spent most of the final year of the war in north Alabama, where it was involved in dozens of operations.[24] John Price Buchanan's son James related a family story that during one encounter with Union troops John Price wheeled his horse to escape the enemy and was whipped across the face by a tree branch. On returning to camp John Price did nothing to dispel the assumption that he had been wounded by the enemy. Only later in his life did he own up to the truth, for which, so the family story goes, he lost out on a Tennessee veteran's pension.[25] The Fourth Alabama Cavalry surrendered in May 1865 at Pond Spring, Alabama, and the unit was disbanded.[26]

There is no documentation on John Price Buchanan's movements immediately after the war, but it seems logical that he would have returned to his father's farm in Williamson County. A J. P. Buchanan signed a legal document as a witness in Williamson County on November 27,

1865, indicating he was home soon after leaving the army.[27] By the fall of that year, a Franklin newspaper reported encouraging developments: "Our town is entirely free from soldiers.... Everything is moving along [at] something like the ante-bellum pace.... Our merchants are doing a prosperous business.... So on the whole, we are getting along amazingly."[28]

Around the same time as the news story, John Price's father, Thomas, had recruited some of his former slaves to work the farm, indicating an expectation that better times were in sight. By the spring of 1866, there was considerable optimism about the recovery of the farm economy. Farm buildings were rebuilt and fencing restored, but crop disease, storms, and flooding in 1866 resulted in poor harvests. As a result the population, particularly the newly freed African Americans, suffered.[29]

POST-WAR MIDDLE TENNESSEE

With the end of the war came the end of slavery, and for all concerned the result was momentous change. As federal troops reached the South, many slaves deserted their masters to follow the troops, join the Union army, or simply try to begin a new life. A rapid and substantial migration of former slaves took place from rural areas to towns and cities.[30] As a result, farm labor was in short supply, a condition that continued long after the war ended.[31]

Initially, white farmers attempted to impose a gang-labor system on their former slaves in order to reimpose a degree of discipline similar to that of slavery.[32] However, the labor shortage permitted African Americans a market advantage that afforded them a bargaining position they had never before enjoyed. They simply refused to accept the working conditions they had endured as slaves. "They demanded shorter work days, less laborious tasks, and more days off; and they declared that black women would no longer work in the fields but in their own homes and gardens as white women did."[33]

Whatever damage was suffered, the records indicate that the Buchanan Williamson County farm remained intact at the end of the war. A most interesting documentation of the transition of slave to paid labor exists in the form of the Freedman's Bureau labor contracts between former slaves and former slave owners.[34] The Bureau of Refugees, Freedmen, and Abandoned Lands, known as the Freedman's Bureau, was created March 3, 1865, as part of the War Department for the purpose of "the supervision and management of all abandoned lands, and the control of all subjects relating to refugees and freedmen from rebel states."[35] The labor contracts were drawn between whites and African Americans, many of whom were former owners and slaves. They specify the terms of working arrangements including the types of labor to be performed, the rate of pay, in-kind payments such as housing and food provisions, relationships between the worker and the employer, and other considerations. These documents, signed by all parties to the agreement and by witnesses, provide an insight into the economy of the post-war community.

With the end of the slave economy, Thomas Buchanan's assets decreased dramatically. However, he negotiated three of these labor contracts with people who most likely had been his slaves. One example follows:

> *Article of agreement between Thomas Buchanan of the one part and Josephus Buchanan and Thomas Wilson (col^d) of the other part all of the county of Williamson State of Tennessee witnesseth that the said Josephus Buchanan and Thomas Wilson by there presents covenants and agrees to work on the farm of said Thomas Buchanan during the whole of the year 1866 and . . . to attend to the feeding of stock and cuting [sic] of fire wood and other duties if required on sundays [sic]. For which services the said Thomas Buchanan covenants and agrees to pay the said Josephus Buchanan and Thomas Wilson the sum of ($125) dollars each during or at the end of the year and find them with plenty of healthy rations.*[36]

In the event that the workers failed to perform their duties, they would be immediately expelled from the property and their wages forfeited unless they were "maltreated."

Thomas also negotiated an agreement between himself and a Daniel Buchanan and his wife Dicey to include their two children. Daniel was to work under the direction of Thomas while Dicey was to perform housework. They were to be paid $175 for the year and be provided a place to live with fuel and food. They were allowed to cultivate their own garden and given time to work the garden and attend to their family's needs. Dicey was to have half the day on Saturday free, and they were allowed "as much as four days during the year to go to Franklin or Nashville."[37] Thomas made a third similar agreement with an Ann Buchanan, who was to work both in the house and on the farm.[38] By today's standards these contracts definitely imposed stringent conditions on the employees, but they constituted marked improvement over the complete absence of rights under slavery. Moreover, the Freedman's Bureau was responsible for monitoring to make sure that the provisions of the contracts were observed.

From such contracts, author Rick Warwick is able to give a picture of the farm economy in Williamson County for 1866. He reports that in order of importance the crops grown were corn, cotton, wheat, oats, tobacco, sorghum, hemp, potatoes, peas, broomcorn, and cabbage.[39]

Given that the Buchanan farm lay close to the area traversed by the Union and Confederate forces during the years of conflict and could have been devastated by the war, these contracts afford a view of the family's fortunes. The labor contracts indicate that Thomas Buchanan was still operating a viable farm in 1865–1866. Despite his reduced circumstances, by 1870 Thomas was again among the more affluent in the county with real estate valued at $7,600 and personal property at $1,500.

The 1870 census reveals two young children still at home, Jennie and James. In addition, there were two teenagers, Martha and Albert Buchanan, who were recorded as living with Thomas and Rebecca Jane though not their children.[40] This census also lists three African-American household members, Ann Wilson (perhaps the one-time Ann Buchanan) and two small children. Ann is identified as a household servant.

Despite the devastation of war and the losses the family suffered, in a relatively short time the Buchanan family was once again faring better than most of its neighbors. Through the generations, the Buchanans had shown themselves to be resourceful, even more capable than those around them.

The post-war changes affected the entire way of life for all middle Tennessee families, including the Buchanans. While the former slaves moved from farm to town, whites moved in the other direction. Between 1860 and 1870 many white middle Tennesseans who had lived in towns and cities moved to farms. One historian concludes that by "1870 white Middle Tennesseans were notably more rural and less urbanized than they had been in 1860."[41]

The migration of former slaves and a smaller farm labor supply dramatically changed the structure of southern agriculture. First, the number of farms increased. Between 1860 and 1870, the number of farms in middle Tennessee increased by about one-third from 19,000 in 1860 to nearly 30,000 in 1870. Second, the farm size fell by nearly 30 percent from an average of 100 acres in 1860 to 71 acres a decade later and to about 40 acres by 1880. Third, before the war just over 20 percent of farms were rented or sharecropped, but by 1870 that percentage had doubled to more than 40 percent.[42] Whereas white tenant farmers more often worked for wages, black farmers typically worked on shares.[43] However, former slaves more commonly worked as farm laborers for wages on land owned and operated by whites, as the example given for Thomas Buchanan and his Freedman's contract illustrates.[44]

Along with changes in farm size and tenancy status, middle Tennessee farmers changed their choice of crops. In an analysis of southern agriculture, historian Robert McKenzie contends that over the 20 years following 1860, corn production in the South fell by 29 percent and swine production by more than 40 percent. He offers the explanation that those farmers switched from the production of foodstuffs to cotton as a cash crop. This shift resulted from the change in farm structure from slave-operated plantations to tenant-operated holdings of 30 to 40 acres.[45] Given the presence of slaves before the War, the Buchanan farm would have been devoted mainly to cotton, as noted earlier. With the loss of the slave labor force, Thomas Buchanan would have had to change his own farm operations.

In the midst of these changes, the Thomas Buchanan family was still on the Williamson County farm in 1880. Jennie Thomas Buchanan, now identified as Tommie, and James were teenagers and still in school. Rebecca Jane died in October 1882 at age 53. The 1890 census records were lost in a fire, but the 1891 Tennessee Voters List includes Thomas living in Williamson County.

Thomas next appears in the 1900 census living in Rutherford County at age 77 with his daughter, Tommie. As of 1900 Thomas continued to identify himself as a farmer owning his own farm and Tommie as a teacher. Both of them died in the fall of 1908 within a month of each other; Thomas was 85 years old and Tommie only 45. M. B. Carter Sr., a lifelong friend of Thomas, wrote an obituary in November 1908 in which he describes his friend: "He was a genial companion, affable, and possessed of all the characteristics that go to make up a gentleman; was scrupulously honest, truthful and fair. . . . If all our people were such as Tom Buchanan, we would have no use for courts, nor law."[46]

There are no surviving records to track his movements

exactly, but sometime after late 1865 Thomas's son John Price moved from Williamson County to neighboring Rutherford County. A number of Buchanan relatives lived in Rutherford County, and certainly he had friends there as well.[47] Soon after arriving in Rutherford County, on his 20th birthday, October 24, 1867, John Price Buchanan married Frances Louise McGill, known as Fannie. As both were children of substantial landowners and influential members of their communities, they were from families of equal social standing, an important factor in that time and place.

The McGill Family

The union between John Price Buchanan and Fannie McGill would have a major impact on the life of the young John Price. His marriage to Fannie made John Price a member of the wealthy, influential McGill family, an association that benefited Buchanan greatly in the future. He now had social standing in both Williamson and Rutherford counties.

Like the Buchanan family, the McGills immigrated to North America from Ireland in the 18th century. William McGill moved to Greene County, Tennessee, in 1785, and his son William moved west to Roane County, Tennessee, in 1802. David McGill, the younger William's son, arrived in Rutherford County in 1819 and became a successful farmer.[48] David and his first wife, Mary McCrary, had six children: John, Elizabeth, James, Nancy, Newton, and Isaac. Mary died in 1842, and David married Isabella Nesbitt in 1849.[49] Following in his father's footsteps, son James became a successful farmer and leading member of the Rutherford County community.

The prominence of the McGill family is evident in the role it played in public affairs in Tennessee. A road network was essential for the development of the regional economy, and the first improved roads in middle Tennessee were developed as private toll roads supervised by the state.[50] In July 1836, the Tennessee General Assembly appointed three commissioners from Rutherford County to organize stock subscriptions for a turnpike from Murfreesboro to Winchester. As replacements for two of the original commissioners, in January 1838 the legislature appointed David McGill and Henry Norman, later to become the father-in-law of David's son James, as commissioners of the Murfreesboro, Manchester, and Winchester Turnpike Company. They were to monitor the company on behalf of the state. Construction of the turnpike progressed quite slowly, and in 1843 the company dropped plans to build the road from Manchester to Winchester, even changing the name accordingly. Still problems continued, and the work was not complete by 1849. Frustrated with the company's problems, the state took control of it in 1852 and appointed James McGill commissioner. The state commissioners were instructed to build a tollgate and hire a gatekeeper to collect tolls.[51]

In 1845 the state legislature incorporated and granted aid to the Nashville and Chattanooga Railroad, on which construction began in 1849. The only established town through which the railroad passed was Murfreesboro. Both the Buchanan and McGill families would have benefited from this new development, since land prices as much as tripled from $5 to $15 per acre within 90 miles of Nashville.[52]

The 1850s were a heady time for both of these families and for middle Tennessee in general.

At the age of 21, James McGill married Margaret Lawrence in 1838, and they had two daughters, Mary J. in 1839 and Sarah Elizabeth McGill in 1840. Sometime after Sarah Elizabeth's birth, Margaret died, and in November 1847 James married Amanda Norman Lowe. Amanda was the widow of Walter S. Lowe of Rutherford County, with whom she had two children, James H. and Elizabeth H. Lowe. In 1848 James and Amanda had their own daughter, Frances Louise McGill.[53] Therefore, in the 1850 census, James and Amanda appear living in southern Rutherford County with five children, three McGill daughters and a Lowe son and daughter. Amanda passed away in November 1852, and with a house full of children James married a third time to Mary Cassandra Norman in about 1853. With Cassie, James fathered two more children, Margaret Catherine and David E. McGill.

By the beginning of the Civil War, James McGill had surpassed his father as a landowner and farmer. The 1860 census reported James owned real estate valued at $40,000 and personal property of more than $26,500. The latter property included 19 slaves, of whom 10 were between 18 and 50 years of age. The settlement of his estate in 1862 indicated that he owned 1,400 acres of land in Rutherford County. Again, the 1860 census reports that David McGill owned 800 acres of land valued at $29,200 with 24 slaves and other property valued at $28,500.[54] The advent of the Civil War brought great tragedy and problems even for this wealthy and privileged family.

James McGill enlisted as a sergeant in Company C

of the 45th Tennessee Infantry Regiment, Confederate, on November 28, 1861. His unit had just been organized at Camp Trousdale, three miles north of today's Portland, Tennessee, then called Richland Station.[55] General Albert Sidney Johnston, who commanded the Confederate Army headquartered in Bowling Green, Kentucky, recognized that Union armies to his east and west substantially outnumbered his forces. Facing this threat the general pressed Tennessee Governor Isham Harris to provide him with more troops. In response the governor initiated the formation of six new Tennessee regiments, including the 45th. A major difficulty in preparing the new regiments for action was the lack of weapons and ammunition. After the beginning of the new year of 1862, the Confederates faced a deteriorating situation. As a last resort the Tennessee legislature authorized the confiscation of private weapons, with promissory notes given to those citizens surrendering their guns. Confederate troops reportedly were armed with "squirrel rifles and shotguns." In mid-January the Confederate army incurred its first significant defeat in the west at Mill Springs, Kentucky, in the Battle of Fishing Creek. As a result the Confederates retreated south and west from Mill Springs in eastern Kentucky. At the same time Union forces commanded by Brigadier General U. S. Grant pressed Johnston's army from the northwest, eventually capturing Forts Henry and Donelson along the Kentucky-Tennessee border on the Tennessee and Cumberland Rivers. Desperate for troops at this point, General Johnston implored Governor Harris for relief.[56]

Here again family stories fill in where there is no documentation of the exact story. First, Robert D. Jamison, a member of McGill's regiment, reports in a letter dated January 30, 1862, to his wife that Company D of the 45th Tennessee Infantry Regiment moved from Camp Trousdale to Bowling Green.[57] It is uncertain whether James McGill and Company C also moved to Kentucky. In early February after Fort Donelson fell to the Union forces, Johnston's remaining troops began a retreat from Bowling Green to Nashville. The weather was reported to be quite severe, and in the course of the retreat nearly a third of the 14,000 Confederates were lost to illness or as stragglers.[58] According to a Buchanan family story, the slave who was sent to retrieve pneumonia-stricken James McGill carried him home on his back.[59] James evidently died in Rutherford County on February 14, 1862.[60] Without confirming evidence we cannot know the exact sequence of events, but either in Kentucky or at Camp Trousdale James McGill, along with many of his fellow soldiers, fell victim to the hazards of army camp life and became ill. At some point, as a man of means, he was able to contact his family about his condition.

Ten days after the death of James McGill in February 1862, Confederate troops retreating from Kentucky, including the 45th Tennessee Regiment, reached Murfreesboro.[61] Within less than a month, federal troops occupied Murfreesboro, and except for a six-month period from July 1862 until January 2, 1863, Murfreesboro was a "captured town." The federal commander, General John Grant Mitchell, required the mayor and aldermen to take the oath of allegiance to the U.S. Constitution, and when Mayor John Dromgoole refused, he was replaced by a pro-Union man. As a result of the failure to officially surrender

Murfreesboro, its inhabitants were not offered much protection or compensation for damages incurred. At the war's end churches, libraries, and schools were in ruin. A minister returned in 1865 to find his church "an utter wreck, nothing standing but the cupola, and the graveyard is also a desolation."[62] In Murfreesboro, Union University, which had been chartered in 1842 and begun operation in 1848, had closed when the war began in 1861.[63] By the end of the war, the campus was in ruin, and the institution was unable to reopen until 1868.[64] The capture and tribulations of Murfreesboro and Rutherford County would affect the McGill family as well as John Price and Fannie Buchanan. However, by the summer of 1865, the McGill farm was operating with a cotton crop in the ground.[65]

James McGill's was a short and bitter experience in the war, and unfortunately the family trials were not over. His father, David, who would have been about 70, died within a month of James's death. While James left a will with instructions for the distribution of his property and provisions for his wife and children, David died leaving no will. By this time Union troops had occupied Nashville, Murfreesboro, and much of northern middle Tennessee, with the result that local governments and courts had ceased to function. David's widow, Isabella, left the farm in 1862 to stay with her own relatives, but she continued to operate the farm with the aid of a farm manager. Because the overseer had health problems, she agreed to let David's son John McGill administer the estate until the courts could clarify the situation.[66] Thus began another family tragedy over the handling of the family's properties.

In 1862, Fannie, Maggie, and young David McGill were

all minors, and guardians represented their interests. The first court records do not appear until 1865, when James McGill's will was probated. At the same time, Isabella McGill, David's wife, charged that John McGill had mishandled the estate and owed it hundreds of dollars. In 1867, James's children, Elizabeth McGill Smith, Maggie McGill, David McGill, and Frances (Fannie) McGill Buchanan, now married to John Price Buchanan, joined Isabella in charging that John or his financial guarantors, or sureties, James Lawrence and Henderson Anderson, owed them nearly $1,000.

The dispute involved a sum of cash the McGill heirs argued was owed to them from transactions conducted during the war years by John McGill. In part the cash derived from a large sale of bacon sold to the Confederates. John McGill responded that the sale had been made for Confederate money, which became worthless after the Union troops took control of the area. However, the postwar courts ruled that debts, even if incurred in Confederate currency, were still valid.[67] The dispute was not settled until 1876, when John McGill was ordered to pay $878.60 to John Price Buchanan and his wife, Fannie; James Robison and his wife, Maggie; and David E. McGill, represented by his guardian, T. J. Elam. Robert P. Smith and his wife, Lizzie, had withdrawn from the suit by this point. John McGill was also ordered to pay Isabella McGill, widow of David McGill, $43.16.[68] The painful episode continued when the sheriff of Coffee County, where John McGill lived, went to enforce the judgment and found that John did not have sufficient money or personal property to pay the amount. Eventually, the court ordered the sale of lands owned by

John McGill and James Lawrence to cover it.[69]

By 1881, Fannie McGill and her husband, John Price Buchanan, had acquired 430 acres from the settlement of the estates of James and David McGill and by purchasing land from other heirs. One piece of that land became theirs as the result of still another sad affair for the McGill family. In August 1879 David E. McGill, the only son of James, was shot and killed while stealing a watermelon as a prank from a neighbor's patch.[70] David was only 22 years old at the time.

The saga of the McGill family was just one of the tragedies for Murfreesboro and middle Tennessee in the wake of the Civil War. The end of the war saw the Buchanan and McGill families in seriously reduced circumstances but not destitute. With the death of David E. McGill, the family name would disappear but not the legacy of his father and grandfather. The Buchanan family, by taking advantage of that legacy, would recover and enter a new period of prosperity and prominence.

NOTES

1. 1850 U.S. Census, Williamson County, 8th Civil District, TN; 1860 U.S. Census, Williamson County, Eastern Subdistrict, TN; 1870 U.S. Census, Williamson County, 8th Civil District, TN.

2. Donald L. Winters, *Tennessee Farming, Tennessee Farmers* (Knoxville, TN: University of Tennessee Press, 1974), pp. 96, 104.

3. 1860 U.S. Census, TN, Williamson County, Eastern Subdistrict, Nolensville P.O., p. 53.

4. Winters, *Tennessee Farming, Tennessee Farmers*, p. 68.

5. The *Central Monitor* (Murfreesboro, TN), Vol. 1, No. 35 (July 12, 1834), reports the call for a meeting to be held on the third Monday of August "to consider the practicality of connecting this place with Columbia by a Railroad."

6. Bonnie L. Gamble, *The Nashville Chattanooga and St. Louis Railroad, 1845–1880: Preservation of a Railroad Landscape*, M.A. Thesis, Middle Tennessee State University, 1993, pp. 7, 31, and 40.

7. Robert E. Corlew, *Tennessee: A Short History*, 2nd ed. (Knoxville, TN: University of Tennessee Press, 1981), p. 206; Kincaid A. Herr, *The Louisville and Nashville Railroad 1850–1940, 1941–1959* (Louisville, KY: *L&N Magazine*, 1959), pp. 27–28.

8. The U.S. National Park Service, Civil War Soldiers and Sailors System database (*http://www.itd.nps.gov/cwss/*) lists two Thomas Buchanan soldiers as having served in the Confederate

Army, but there is no application for Thomas Buchanan in the Tennessee Veterans Pension database (*http://www.tennessee. gov/tsla/history/military/pension.htm*). The record of John Price Buchanan is discussed below.

9. Jonathan Atkins, "Politicians, Parties, and Slavery: The Second Party System and the Decision for Disunion in Tennessee," in *Tennessee History: The Land, the People, and the Culture*, ed. Carroll Van West (Knoxville, TN: University of Tennessee Press, 1998), p. 140.

10. Mary French Caldwell, *Tennessee: The Volunteer State* (Chicago, IL: Richtext Press, 1968), p. 110, and Bergeron et al., *Tennesseans and Their History*, p. 135.

11. Rick Warwick, *Williamson County, The Civil War Years Revealed through Letters, Diaries & Memoirs* (Franklin, TN: Heritage Foundation of Franklin and Williamson County, 2006), p. 6.

12. Stephen V. Ash, *Middle Tennessee Society Transformed 1860–1870: War and Peace in the Upper South* (Baton Rouge, LA: Louisiana State University Press, 1988), p. 80.

13. Ibid., p. 227.

14. Ibid., p. 151.

15. Ibid., p. 86.

16. Ibid., p. 87.

17. Ibid., p. 163.

18. Shelby Foote, *The Civil War, A Narrative, Red River to Appomattox* (New York: Vintage Books, 1986), pp. 674, 708.

19. Gamble, "The Nashville, Chattanooga, and St. Louis Railroad," pp. 115–116. James H. Grant, W. S. Huggins, and T. C. Whiteside, "Report of the Special Committee," in *Annual Report 1866* by Nashville, Chattanooga, and St. Louis Railroad (Nashville, TN: Roberts, Waterson, and Purvis, 1866), pp. 17–21 (Tennessee State Library and Archives).

20. Stephen V. Ash, *Middle Tennessee Society Transformed 1860–1870: War and Peace in the Upper South*. Baton Rouge, LA: Louisiana State University Press, 1988), p. 175.

21. John Price Buchanan was possibly named for his mother's great-grandfather John Price. Often the middle name given in that generation was from the maternal line.

22. Carol Hoffman, "John Price Buchanan—Farmer and Politician," *Rutherford County Historical Society Publication*, No. 21, Summer 1983.

23. "Soldier's Application for Pension" filed March 22, 1929 (Tennessee State Library and Archives).

24. *http://www.geocities.com/Athens/Aegean/6349/actions.htm*, retrieved August 16, 2012.

25. Carol Hoffman, Appendix 2, p. 98; interview with James M. Buchanan Jr. and John Whorley Jr. in Indianapolis, IN, May 16, 2007.

26. *Biographical Directory, Tennessee General Assembly 1796–*

1967 (Preliminary No. 6), Rutherford County (Nashville, TN: Tennessee State Library and Archives).

27. Rick Warwick, *Freedom and Work in the Reconstruction Era: The Freedmen's Bureau Labor Contracts of Williamson County, Tennessee* (Heritage Foundation of Franklin and Williamson County, TN, 2006), #143, p. 94. The document is a labor agreement between Thomas H. Peebles and two of his former slaves. It is possible that this J. P. Buchanan is not John Price, as there was another Buchanan family in Williamson County, though no one with those initials appeared in the 1860 census.

28. Ash, *Middle Tennessee Society Transformed*, p. 183.

29. Ibid., pp. 185–186.

30. Ibid., p. 183.

31. Robert Tracy McKenzie, *One South or Many? Plantation Belt and Upcountry in Civil War-Era Tennessee* (New York: Cambridge University Press, 2002), pp. 155–156.

32. Ibid., p. 186.

33. Ibid., p. 186.

34. Warwick, *Freedom and Work*.

35. Corlew, *Tennessee: A Short History*, pp. 339–340; *http://www.history.umd.edu/Freedmen/fbact.htm*, retrieved August 16, 2012.

36. Warwick, *Freedom and Work*, p. 91, agreement 136.

37. Ibid., pp. 132–133, agreement 259.

38. Ibid., p. 133, agreement 260.

39. Ibid., p. 2.

40. From the family records presented in the previous chapter, it does not appear that Martha and Albert Buchanan were Thomas's niece and nephew, but the extended Buchanan family was very large by 1870, and these children could have come from a family not located in Williamson County.

41. Ash, *Middle Tennessee Society Transformed*, p. 237.

42. Ibid., pp. 152, 187.

43. McKenzie, *One South or Many?*, pp. 133–135.

44. Ibid., p. 137.

45. McKenzie, *One South or Many?*, pp. 134, 172.

46. Obituary of Thomas Buchanan, *Review Appeal*.

47. The half brother of Major John Buchanan, Moses Ridley Buchanan, operated one of the first gristmills in Rutherford County with his uncle, Moses Ridley, according to Carlton C. Sims, *A History of Rutherford County* (Murfreesboro, TN: Carlton C. Sims, 1947), p. 60. A Richard Buchanan, who may have been related, is reported to have been a founding member of a Murfreesboro chapter of the Independent Order of Odd Fellows in 1845. See John C. Spence, *Annals of Rutherford County*, Vol. 2: 1829–1870 (Nashville, TN: Williams Printing Company, 1991).

48. Family genealogical records.

49. Susan Daniel, *Cemeteries and Graveyards of Rutherford County, Tennessee* (Murfreesboro, TN: Rutherford County Historical Society, 2005), p. 355.

50. In Williamson County, John Buchanan was entangled in a lawsuit over damage to his property involving the Franklin Turnpike Company. The suit was filed sometime in 1829, and a settlement was not reached until April 1834, when John Buchanan was nearing death. *Williamson County Court Minutes*, Vol. 12, pp. 319, 352, 377, 538, and Vol. 13, pp. 447, 447, 516.

51. Edward C. Annable Jr., "A History of the Roads of Rutherford County Tennessee, 1804–1878," M.A. Thesis, Middle Tennessee State University (December 1982); *Rutherford County Historical Society Publication*, No. 20, pp. 56–59.

52. Gamble, "The Nashville, Chattanooga, and St. Louis Railroad," pp. 31–32.

53. In some records Frances is spelled with an *i* and sometimes with an *e*.

54. *Rutherford County, Tennessee Court, Record Book*, 21, pp. 193–195 (Rutherford County, TN Archives); *1860 U.S. Census and Slave Schedule*, p. 22.

55. Tennessee Historical Commission, *Tennesseans in the Civil War, Part I: A Military History of the Confederate and Union Units with Available Rosters of Personnel* (Civil War Commission: 1964), p. 273. Richland Station was a stop on the Louisville & Nashville (L&N) Railroad. The site of the camp remains undevel-

oped farmland, and in 2006 Governor Phil Bredesen of Tennessee proposed preserving the site. Portland is about 35 miles north of Nashville.

56. *The War of the Rebellion: A Compilation of the Official Records of the Union and Confederate Armies*, Series I, Vol. VII, Ch. XVII, pp. 769, 779, 781, 794–795, 811–812, 827–828, 845.

57. Robert David Jamison, *Letters and Recollections of a Confederate Soldier, 1860–1865* (Nashville, TN: H. D. Jamison, 1964). An advertisement in *Murfreesboro Weekly News*, Vol. X, No. 17 (April 30, 1880) names R. D. Jamison as president of Union University in Murfreesboro.

58. William Preston Johnston, *The Life of General Albert Sidney Johnston* (New York: D. Appleton & Co., 1878), p. 493.

59. Interview with the Buchanan family in October 2006.

60. James McGill is buried along with many others from the McGill and Buchanan families in the Mt. Tabor Cumberland Presbyterian Church graveyard next to the John Price Buchanan School, about three miles south of Murfreesboro, TN, on U.S. Highway 41 South.

61. *Tennesseans in the Civil War*, Vol. 1, p. 273.

62. Ash, *Middle Tennessee Society Transformed*, p. 175.

63. Carlton C. Sims, ed., *A History of Rutherford County* (Nashville, TN: Tennessee Historical Commission, 1947), p. 152. In listing presidents for Soule College, which Methodists opened in Murfreesboro in 1853 and which appears to have provided one

to two years of college work, Sims, p. 154, does not list a president for the years 1863–1865, suggesting it must have closed during this time.

64   Ibid., pp. 178–179. Union was later merged with other schools and moved to Jackson, Tennessee, where it was initially named Southwestern Baptist University but today bears the Union University name.

65. Deposition of John McGill, *Minute Book*, Rutherford County Chancery Court, May 31, 1877 (Rutherford County Archives).

66. Deposition of Isabella McGill, *Minutes Book*, Rutherford County Chancery Court, August 21, 1869 (Rutherford County Archives).

67. Ash, *Middle Tennessee Society Transformed*, fn. 11, p. 181.

68. *Minute Book*, Rutherford County Chancery Court, April Term 1876, pp. 298–299 (Rutherford County Archives).

69. *Minute Book*, Rutherford County Chancery Court, April 3, 1877 (Rutherford County Archives).

70. Per family story from interview of James M. Buchanan Jr. and Elizabeth Buchanan Bradley in Blacksburg, VA, December 1, 2006.

CHAPTER V.

JOHN PRICE BUCHANAN AND THE AGRARIAN REVOLT

In 1873, 26-year-old John Price and 25-year-old Fannie Buchanan moved to the Big Creek Stock Farm, which would be their home for more than 50 years. Buchanan raised livestock on 185 acres along the Manchester Pike.[1] Despite the difficult times of the 1870s and 1880s, John P. Buchanan became a successful farmer like his father and forebears. In addition, he developed another facet of life by entering the realm of politics in a turbulent period of American history.

THE FARMERS' DISCONTENT

The South had suffered physical and economic ruin from the Civil War.[2] An 1872 congressional investigation estimated that Tennessee alone had suffered a loss of $185 million from the war.[3] By way of comparison, the total revenue of the federal government in 1872 was $374 million.[4] The war imposed huge economic costs on both the North and the South, but economic historians argue that by 1879 the North, consisting of those states that constituted the Union of 1861, had recovered in terms of per capita consumption. In contrast, by 1879 the South had not achieved even three-quarters of the level of per capita consumption of 1860.[5] Economic historian Peter Temin argues that the differences in the experiences between the North and the South are explained by three factors: the end of slavery and the accompanying decline in the quantity of labor supplied, the physical destruction and dislocation resulting from the war, and a decline in the demand for cotton, still the South's main cash crop.[6]

The 1870s and 1880s saw great expansion of the American West and important technological changes in farming techniques.[7] In Tennessee the amount of improved land used in farming increased from 6.8 million acres in 1870 to nearly 8.5 million in 1880.[8] Accompanying the growing cultivation of land was an increase in the number of persons engaged in farming in Tennessee. In 1870 the number of people identifying their occupation as agriculture totaled 267,000. In 1880 that number increased to 294,000, and by 1890 the total was more than 336,000.[9] The increase in the number of farms, the westward expansion of the country, and the introduction of new farming technologies resulted in falling crop and land prices.

The national economy experienced a number of contractions following the Civil War, most significantly the longest contraction in the history of the U.S. economy, between October 1873 and March 1879.[10] Between 1870 and the mid-1890s, the price of cotton fell from more than 20 cents per pound to less than five cents, when a price of eight cents per pound was thought to be the breakeven price for farmers.[11]

One analysis of Tennessee agriculture in the post–Civil War years shows a dramatic decline in the median value of production per farm between 1859 and 1879, even after adjusting for inflation. As a result farm incomes declined along with the decrease in farm size.[12] McKenzie compares farm incomes of 1880 with the value of food and other items consumed by "the typical Tennessee slave in 1859" and concludes that many Tennessee farm families, particularly in east and middle Tennessee, would have subsisted on less than the average antebellum slave.[13]

Adding to the problem of falling farm incomes was an increase in competition for fertile land. It may seem a contradiction that increased competition for land would coincide with falling land prices, but in addition to the demand for farmland, the price of that land is also determined by expected future prices of farm products. As a result falling crop prices led to lower land prices. In the face of these forces during the late 19th century, many young farmers in middle Tennessee entered an extremely crowded agricultural sector. Thus, farmers were squeezed between falling crop prices and obtaining enough farm acreage to support their families.[14]

Rutherford County, Tennessee, tax records indicate that the assessed value of the Buchanan farmland declined by more than 63 percent between 1877 and 1887.[15] That fact alone may have inspired John Price Buchanan to look for political solutions to his losses, and at this point he began his controversial career in the politics of Tennessee and the country.

Before the war, farm families provided for their own needs first and used any surplus to participate in the commercial economy. With declining prices and incomes, farmers felt themselves exploited by the development of new economic forces, namely the railroads and the rise of the corporation.

Latter-day economists and historians have argued that despite perceptions of the period real incomes did not fall in the 1880s and 1890s. The prices farmers paid for goods and services used and consumed, including freight and interest rates, fell faster than the prices received for their crops.[16] What then motivated the complaints of traditionally conservative farmers and the rise of their political activism? One argument is that farmers and farm families were pressed to participate in a market economy that imposed relentless demands over which they had little control. Economic historian Anne Mayhew offers the hypothesis that rather than being "mad at 'monopolists,' 'middlemen,' and 'moneylenders,'" they were mad at the commercialization of their lives. "The argument is that the farmers were objecting to the *increasing importance of prices*; that they were protesting a system in which they had to pay for transport and money rather than the specific *prices* of transport and money."[17]

Whereas pioneer farm families had provided much of the food and other materials necessary for everyday living, in the post-war period farm families *bought* newly developed seeds, fertilizer, manufactured farm equipment, and blooded livestock and paid for them in cash or on credit.[18] Even the smallest farmers were drawn into commercial agriculture with the risks of market fluctuation. The "coercion" of the market imposed an unwelcome discipline on farm families.

A group of Rutherford County farmers protested what

they perceived to be a meatpackers' monopoly organized by the Armour Company. They argued that the corporations were able "to send ready-dressed beef into Tennessee cities to take markets from local stock-raisers, who then had to ship their beef to Chicago, St. Louis, 'or whatever other place those cursed, heartless, cut throats may designate, and then be forced to sell for the cost of raising.'"[19]

Middle Tennessee farmers had desired to participate in the commercial economy from their arrival a century earlier. As early as the first years of settlement, the Buchanan family and others were ready to sell their crops outside the Cumberland region. By the time of the Civil War, middle Tennessee farm owners produced at least 50 percent more than they consumed. In 1860 Nashville, the most populous city of the region, with a population of 17,000, could not have consumed all of the surplus food produced in middle Tennessee. Before and after the war, area farmers supplied pork and beef to the mid-south and other areas of the country.[20]

In an analysis of farm incomes, one historian reports that farmers participating in the market economy earned up to five times as much as subsistence farmers. In his view, any desire to avoid the pressures of the market was mistaken. "The evidence is compelling that poverty, rather than independence, was the real reward of those truly isolated from the market."[21]

Whatever the case, unrest among farmers over the conditions they faced grew and was evident in the rise of farm-based organizations.[22] In the 1880s farmers' discontent intensified, and more assertive groups rose to advocate the cause of the improvement of farm life. John Price Buchanan would play a major role in the movement spawned by this discontent.

In February 1882, a number of Arkansas farmers organized the Agricultural Wheel to take political action against what they saw as economic injustice. The name was adopted to reflect the founders' view that agriculture was the "wheel" of the national economy. An Arkansas State Wheel was organized in 1883, followed by the National Agricultural Wheel in July 1884. The first Tennessee Wheel was founded in Weakley County in February 1884, and with 154 locals in five west Tennessee counties the Tennessee State Wheel was chartered in July 1885. When the last state Wheel met in Clarksville in 1888 before merging with another group, the organization claimed 42,000 members in 42 Tennessee counties.[23]

In 1887, the Wheel held a national convention in McKenzie, Tennessee. John H. McDowell, outspoken advocate for the Wheel positions and editor of the organization's publication, the *Weekly Toiler*, chaired a committee to formulate the group's policy concerns. The convention adopted 14 demands that reappear in the platform of John Price Buchanan in later years.[24] These demands included

- paying off the national debt,
- repealing laws that favored capital over labor,
- preventing aliens from owning land,
- abolishing national banks,
- operating government on a cash basis,
- ending agricultural futures trading,
- establishing a graduated income tax,
- prohibiting importation of foreign labor,

- national ownership of transportation and communication,
- direct election of national politicians,
- free trade and removal of all import duties,
- establishing a luxury tax,
- free public education, and
- no renewal of patents.

The convention also resolved that "this body will not support any man for Congress, of any political party, who will not pledge himself in writing, to use all his influence for the formation of these demands into laws."[25] In 1877, a small group of Texas farmers met to discuss their problems and formed the Knights of Reliance, which was subsequently renamed the Texas Farmers' Alliance and spread to other states. Through the 1880s the organization grew dramatically, voicing its concerns over excessive costs of farm supplies and the falling price of cotton. One spokesman for the alliance asserted that farmers' problems could be laid at the feet of the manipulative capitalist, who "holds your confidence in one hand, while with the other he rifles your pocket."[27]

With the aid of a national organizer, the first Farmers' Alliance group in Tennessee met in Wilson County in 1887. The ideas of the Alliance must have found fertile ground because a year later the Tennessee Farmers' Alliance held a statewide convention. John Price Buchanan, now a Rutherford County cattle raiser, led the convention. As will be discussed below, Buchanan by this point had entered politics and was a member of the Tennessee General Assembly.

Both the Wheel and the Alliance promoted farmers'

cooperatives as a means of reducing costs and loosening the hold of business interests. They organized state and county cooperative buying agencies to purchase farm equipment and staples and then resold them at discounted prices to co-op members. This effort extended to forming sellers' co-ops to market cotton, tobacco, and peanuts, with the objective of obtaining higher prices for member farmers. In his address to the state convention in 1889, John Price Buchanan, then president of the Tennessee Alliance, stated that "we had but little co-operation in our organization in Tennessee, until we adopted the State Agency system; this, though still in its infancy, has worked wonders for the general interest of those engaged in agricultural pursuits. . . . Co-operation is the key that unlocks our future."[28]

Merchants and retailers attempted to resist the cooperative approach by filing lawsuits to force the taxation of co-ops as ordinary business enterprises, but the courts did not agree with the plaintiffs' argument.[29] During the election of 1890, conflict between the business community and the Alliance-supported cooperatives threatened to embarrass Buchanan, the Democratic nominee for governor.[30]

In a prelude to the political successes of 1888 and 1890, Tennessee farmers and their organizations combined against one of their common "enemies." In 1888 the St. Louis firm of Warren, Jones, and Gratz, a distributor of jute bagging used for cotton, with a 25-percent market share, organized a cartel that raised the price from 6.5 to 12.5 cents per yard in July of that year. The effect was to unite farmers, cotton planters, and merchants against the cartel. A collaboration of Wheel and Alliance groups sustained a boycott of jute bagging until jute prices dropped in the fall of 1889.[31]

JOHN PRICE BUCHANAN, FARMER-POLITICIAN

In this climate of anger and political struggle, the Buchanan name became associated with the movement known variously as the farmers' discontent or Populism. John Price Buchanan's political career began with unsuccessful efforts to run for local office in Rutherford County. As an advocate for farm interests, he appeared first in 1881 chairing a Rutherford County meeting to support low taxes.[32] In 1881 the legislature passed a bill to fund the state debt at its full face value with three-percent bonds, known as the 100–3 bill. Rutherford County Democrats met to protest the Republican-sponsored law, and the meeting, chaired by John Price Buchanan, resolved that it "was a step toward serfdom."[33]

In 1886 Buchanan was elected to the first of two terms in the Tennessee General Assembly.[34] Thus, his political career began before his rise in the Alliance. Despite his reputation for being a simple farmer unable to speak in public, he clearly established himself as a community leader and respected spokesmen for state farmers well in advance of his run for governor.

As a legislator Buchanan began modestly, but he advanced issues that he championed throughout his political career. During his first term, he introduced a veterans' pension bill to assist those wounded during the war. He supported public education with a petition to the legislature to redistrict counties into school districts.[35]

While he was establishing his reputation as a politician, Buchanan's standing among activist farmers rose dramatically. The Wheel and the Farmers' Alliance joined forces

Figure 9. 47th Tennessee General Assembly, 1891–1892

in July 1889 to form the Farmers' and Laborers' Union, typically referred to as the Alliance, of which John Price Buchanan was unanimously elected state president.[36] The new organization consisted of 99,000 members.[37] It distinguished itself from other bodies by excluding certain groups from membership. For example, membership was limited to "farmers, farm laborers, country school teachers, country ministers of the gospel, country doctors and country mechanics and excluded a postmaster and member of the Wheel."[38]

Consequently, occupation was a defining aspect of membership in this farm-centered group. Community standing was determined by a complex mixture of family, church, profession, property ownership, membership in organizations such as the Masons, and other factors. Economic position was not an essential factor. While a postmaster and a bank manager might be excluded, a substantial landowner would not. In fact, in Rutherford County the leading Alliancemen had farms larger than the typical farm of the area.[39] Over the years 1873 through 1890, John Price and Fannie Buchanan added land to their farm up to a total of 430 acres; the Big Creek Stock Farm was no run-of-the-mill place.

When John Price Buchanan, a member of the Cumberland Presbyterian church, assumed his duties as president of the Alliance, he related the duties of the membership to their religious obligations by noting "there are no three greater duties of practical Christianity, than to strive for the interests of one's own household, and for the interests of one's fellow laborers, and for the interests of one's fellow citizens."[40]

Nostalgia for the "Lost Cause," a romantic notion that developed in the decade after the Civil War, was another element in the political climate of the post-war South.[41] Many members of the Farmers' Alliance were Confederate veterans. Democrats used the allegiance of the veterans to their memories of the war to attract them to vote for party candidates. This allegiance worked for and against the Alliance candidates.[42]

John Price Buchanan always promoted the interests of Confederate veterans. With the recovery of the vote and the subsequent capture of state governments, Southern Democrats began retrenchment from the policies the Radical Republicans instituted following the war. As a politician, Buchanan was a man of his time and place, and efforts to disenfranchise African-American voters were a part of the politics of the era. Examples of laws that tended to eliminate blacks from voter rolls in Tennessee were the Dortch Law, the Myers Law, and the Lea Law, not to mention the poll tax.[43] Senator Josiah H. Dortch sponsored a bill in 1890 requiring voters to mark and deposit their ballots in secret, which in effect barred illiterate voters from the electoral process. Representative Thomas R. Myers of Bedford County, Speaker of the House, sponsored a bill to require voter registration in all towns and districts with more than 2,500 people. The law also required each voter to present a valid registration certificate when he cast his ballot. The Lea Law, named for Senator Benjamin J. Lea, Speaker of the Senate, required separate ballot boxes for state and federal elections; this law was repealed in 1891.[44] These laws were a part of what became known as Jim Crow laws, which were common in the South by the end of the 19th century and prevented blacks from voting in any elections.[45]

The Gubernatorial Election of 1890

Historian Roger Hart describes Tennessee post–Civil War politics as a four-way division among those concerned with national versus local issues and mercantile versus agrarian interests. The cotton planters of west Tennessee, characterized as Bourbons, were interested in local, mercantile issues. Unionist east Tennessee was concerned with national agrarian issues, while middle Tennesseans, including hardscrabble farmers on the eastern rim, merchants and manufacturers from Nashville, and farmers from the fertile Central Basin, constituted a mixture of all groups.[46]

The election of 1888 provides clear evidence of the agrarian revolt in Tennessee. In November of that year, the *Weekly Toiler* reported that 41 of 132 state legislators were members of the Wheel or the Farmers' Alliance. Among them was John Price Buchanan, elected to his second term in the General Assembly.[47] The political advocates of the farmers introduced legislation in January 1889 to exempt the state cooperative agency from business taxes. Representative Buchanan was instrumental in getting the bill passed. During his second term he sponsored bills to modify the state constitution, regulate banking, amend the law apportioning congressional districts, and exempt agricultural agents from the privilege tax. In particular he took seriously the management of state government in an efficient and businesslike manner.[48] The stage was then set for a takeover by the farmers.

Four candidates competed for the Democratic nomination for governor in 1890. First, Jere Baxter of Davidson County was a former president of the Memphis and

Charleston Railroad who raised thoroughbred racehorses. In an effort to demonstrate his allegiance to farm issues, he joined the Alliance, but the membership did not recognize him as a true Allianceman. Baxter received support from New South Democrats, who advocated industrial development and the adoption of modern farming technologies.[49]

Bourbon Democrats offered Josiah Patterson of Memphis as their candidate. Patterson was a native of Alabama, a veteran of Forrest's cavalry, and a lawyer. Like Baxter he tried to attract the farm vote.[50] A third candidate, also an attorney, was another west Tennessean from Henderson County, John M. Taylor. While Taylor had some standing with farmers, it did not extend beyond his own region of the state.

John Price Buchanan, member of the General Assembly and president of the Farmers' and Laborers' Union, was the fourth candidate. The *Weekly Toiler* commended him as a "self-made man," "a prosperous farmer and stock raiser," and a "splendid parliamentarian." While Buchanan was never a member of the political establishment, in the eyes of his fellow Alliance members he was clearly their leader and up to the job.[51]

Many newspapers around the state greeted Buchanan's candidacy with derision. One editor who misspelled his name sneered, "The idea of J. P. having any of the symptoms of a statesman borders somewhat on the ludicrous." Critics called him "highly hilarious" and referred to him as an "alleged candidate for Governor."[52]

Despite the skepticism of the party establishment, Buchanan began to score victories in county conventions and primaries prior to the state convention. A reporter for the *Manchester Times* observed, "The farmers of Tennessee seem to be getting in their work pretty well judging from the number of counties which are instructed for Buchanan." John Taylor went so far as to adopt the entire Farmers' Alliance platform as his own, demonstrating the strength of Buchanan's candidacy.[53]

The state Democratic convention opened on July 15, 1890. On the first ballot Buchanan led with more than twice the votes of the second leading candidate, Josiah Patterson, but convention rules required a two-thirds majority for nomination. Despite calls to release delegates to vote their own convictions, the leaders of the Farmers' Alliance maintained discipline among their ranks to hold fast to their support for Buchanan.[54] The contest lasted until the other candidates finally withdrew, John Taylor on the 24th ballot and Baxter and Patterson on the 26th.[55]

Throughout the campaign the establishment candidates and their supporters among newspaper editors painted Buchanan as a member of a secret society, i.e., the Farmers' Alliance, seeking to advance farmers over the rest of the populace, rather than as a loyal Democrat. To dispute this contention, in his acceptance speech Buchanan vowed to fight for "the great principles enunciated by Jackson, Polk, and Johnson."[56] In an interview with the *Nashville Daily American*, he was adamant on this point:

> *I am making this campaign as a Democrat on a Democratic platform. I have never urged anybody to support me because I was an alliance man or a farmer. . . . It is a grave mistake to suppose, as some do, that I am seeking to array one class against another, or that I*

want to benefit the agricultural at the expense of other interests.[57]

His hometown friends and supporters greeted his return to Murfreesboro with a procession. Wagons lined the street at the train depot festooned with banners that read "Andrew Johnson from the tailor's bench; Buchanan from the plow," or "It is not wealth, nor pomp, nor state, but git up and git that makes a man great."[58]

In September 1890, Buchanan gave his first campaign speech in Franklin, in his native Williamson County. The editor of the *Nashville Banner* panned the speech as lacking "original suggestions or vigorous discussion."[59] As the Democratic candidate, Buchanan advocated more equitable taxes, support for education, better roads, and "the development of resources without abuses by capitalists."[60] He held that "in all Governments there are two forces, the force of the centralizing power and the force of the will of the people." He asserted that the centralizers were winning in the form of national Republicans, whom he likened to Imperial Rome, favoring monopoly and high tariffs.[61]

In the general election, Republican Lewis T. Baxter, a Nashville real estate man, and the Reverend D. C. Kelley, the Prohibition Party nominee, opposed Buchanan.[62] Baxter injected the race issue into the campaign when he opposed a national Republican bill before Congress that called for federal oversight of voter registration and elections when requested by local petitioners. His position split Tennessee Republicans and solidified Democratic loyalty.[63]

Election Day was November 4, 1890, and Buchanan received 56.6 percent of the vote, with his Republican

Figure 10. Governor John Price Buchanan

opponent receiving 37.9 percent and the Prohibition candidate getting 5.5 percent.[64] Buchanan was one of six governors elected in 1890 who were members of the Farmers' Alliance. Fifty-four Alliance members were elected to the Tennessee legislature, giving them a substantial vote in both houses of the legislature.[65]

In his inaugural address Governor Buchanan expressed much of his basic philosophy of government. First, government had made "dangerous strides toward plutocracy by submission to the power of aggregated money. . . . It has by these errors fostered monopoly until it has placed itself within the merciless grasp of this relentless tyrant." Second, Tennessee did not require new laws; it needed only to efficiently enforce those on the books. Third, while state government might encourage economic development, a Buchanan administration would seek growth that benefited all: "Progress does not mean a mushroom growth of 'booms' and wild speculation in which a few are enriched to the detriment of the many."[66] These sentiments were themes that Buchanan repeated throughout his political career.

Over the first weeks of his administration, Governor Buchanan received praise for his appointments and work ethic. Only his appointment of his political mentor, John McDowell, then president of the Alliance and ardent spokesman for farm issues, as coal oil inspector brought complaints. Opponents immediately charged that the appointment was a political payoff. The hostile *Nashville Banner* called for a lowering of coal oil fees and diminution of the inspector's position. The appointment divided Alliance members.[67]

As governor, Buchanan did not urge any particular program on the legislature. Instead he let them set the agenda. His only instruction to them was to do their duty:

> *In whatever will make our fields more productive, our manufactures more numerous, our business more prosperous, the investment of our capital more secure, the rewards of labor more remunerative and just; in whatever will lighten and equalize the burdens of taxation, make stronger the State Government, benefit and ele-*

vate the masses of the people, you will have my hearty sympathy and best efforts.[68]

Critics of the farmer-legislators charged that they had no agenda. Almost immediately, the old-line Democrats asserted their power, and often the Alliancemen followed their lead.[69]

There were some issues that most concerned farmers and spurred them to action. The legislature had created in 1871 the Bureau of Agriculture, Statistics, Mines, and Immigration. With the bureau's having such a broad charge, farmers argued that the interests of agriculture were subordinated to those of mining and manufacturing. In 1891, Governor Buchanan recommended, and the legislature subsequently created, a Bureau of Labor to consolidate the activities of statistics and mines, separate from a Bureau of Agriculture.[70]

Another issue that concerned farmers and Buchanan was the state of agricultural education in the state. For some time, Tennessee farmers had criticized the University of Tennessee for its emphasis on a liberal arts curriculum to the exclusion of a more pragmatic course of study that would directly benefit future farmers. The farmers complained they paid taxes for an institution that did not benefit them. A second complaint was that the university was located in the eastern part of the state and that even when agricultural programs were available, they were not relevant to farmers in middle and west Tennessee.[71]

Another long-term issue with farmers was the conduct of railroads. On this issue there was some agreement across the spectrum of Democratic factions.[72] Particularly among farmers the perception was that the complicated railroad tariffs cheated and discriminated against them. Numerous examples of rail rates gave this impression. Grain shipped from Nashville to Atlanta cost 20 cents per hundred-weight (cwt), while a Murfreesboro shipper paid 24 cents, though the distance was 30 miles shorter. Whiskey shipped 11 miles from Bradford to Milan, Tennessee, cost $4.05 and then $3.60 for the 400 miles from Milan to Cincinnati, Ohio.[73]

A Tennessee railroad commission had been created in 1883 but imposed little regulation on railroads, and the authorizing law was repealed in 1885.[74] Tennessee farmers generally did not oppose railroads, but the Wheel and the Farmers' Alliance opposed state subsidy for railroads. Alliance members opposed "taxing individuals for the benefit of corporations." Governor Buchanan issued his first veto to stop the appropriation of money to support railroad construction.[75] However, Tennessee farmers did not press for railroad regulation. In contrast to other states with strong Alliance movements, neither the farmer-dominated Tennessee legislature nor its farmer-governor supported legislation that would have created a new regulatory commission.[76]

A final farm-related issue concerned taxation. Tennessee had incurred substantial public debt supporting the construction of railroads during the period of Reconstruction following the Civil War. Low-tax Democrats opposed paying the entire face value of the debt, and they offered a number of schemes for partial payment over the 1880s to deal with the issue. Basically, the farmers saw taxation for debt service as favoring the wealthy financiers of the railroads. The matter became problematic for the Buchanan-era government. A revenue bill introduced at the end of the legislative session of 1891 contained an increase in the privilege tax on corporations. The proposed bill raised the tax rate and apportioned taxes on the basis of population, which larger towns and counties regarded as discriminatory, and exempted agricultural associations from the tax. Historian Connie Lester states, "Clearly, the bill pitted agrarian interests against commercial and industrial concerns."[77] The bill was defeated on the floor of the House. A second version passed, and whether it was justified or not, the Alliance took the blame for promoting class warfare. Historian Lester assessed the impact as negative for the governor and the Alliance:

> *The timing of the bill (at the very end of the legislative session), the haste with which a new bill was prepared (after weeks of work on the original bill), the previous lack of radicalism on the part of Alliance legislators, and the complete capitulation of the measure in favor of reduced rates suggest that the first bill represented a political maneuver rather than a serious attempt to pass a revenue bill. Alliance foes successfully tied the organization to the measure while offering no evidence to support their accusations. In the minds of many Tennesseans, the Farmers' Alliance became the anti-industry, anticommerce, anti-urban naysayers that voters had always feared.*[78]

Here was a major blow to the farmer-legislators and another mark against Governor John Price Buchanan.

The governor and the Alliance legislature were credited

with some positive achievements. An 1873 bill calling for publicly funded primary education was amended to include secondary schools as well. At the time, primary schools covered grades one through five, while secondary schools covered grades six through eight. In his 1891 address to the legislature, Governor Buchanan urged passage of an education bill:

> *The duty of the State to educate her children is no longer a debatable question. . . . The requirements of citizenship in so complex a government as ours makes public education a necessity. . . . Tennessee needs the brain power of the masses of her people, and should not be frugal in this use of her means.*[79]

A section of the education reform bill that was passed promoted a course in "Elementary Principles of Agriculture" to be offered in the newly supported public secondary schools. Along with the extension of state support for education, Buchanan proposed setting qualifications for county school superintendents as well as studying methods to provide textbooks to all students. In addition, he recommended assuring the salary of the state superintendent of public instruction. Up to that point the salary apparently had been paid at the discretion of the legislature.[80] The legislature supported teacher education by increasing its appropriations for the Peabody Normal School and for summer teacher training institutes.[81]

True to Buchanan's support for Confederate veterans, the legislature instituted monthly pensions of up to $25 for disabled veterans. The construction and maintenance of the Tennessee Confederate Soldiers' Home was funded for $35,000.[82]

THE COAL MINERS' STRIKE

The summer of 1891 marked the beginning of a series of events that effectively doomed the active political career of John Price Buchanan. Following the Civil War, Tennessee was broke and had no resources to provide for a penal system. In consequence the Tennessee legislature adopted a system, first instituted in 1846 by the state of Alabama, by which the state penitentiary leased prisoners to private businesses in return for a fee and responsibility for feeding and housing the convicts.[83] The first Tennessee convicts leased under the system in 1866 went to a furniture company, but other businesses began to lease prisoners as well.

The leasing system was extremely harsh, and for African Americans, who made up the largest share of the convict population, it was highly abusive. The prison system was brutal, and prison guards often treated the inmates inhumanely. Under the lease system conditions were no better. One Southern businessman observed, "Before the war, we owned the negroes. If a man had a good negro, he could afford to keep him. . . . But these convicts, we don't own 'em. One dies, get another."[84]

Problems began by 1871 over convicts leased to coal-mining companies. Soon the largest leaser of Tennessee convicts was the Tennessee Coal, Iron, and Railroad Company, better known as TCI. Coal mining was a seasonal business, and during the summer months the mines were shut down and miners laid off, eliminating any bargaining strength they may have had. Then in the fall when the mines reopened, the miners were called back. Free white miners in Tracy City, Grundy County, Tennessee, went on strike in 1871, demanding a wage increase and an end to the use of convict labor. Wage-earning miners protested having to work alongside convicts in 1877 by setting off three kegs of powder under the convicts' barracks. Clearly the convict-leasing system was contentious and violent from its beginnings, long before John Price Buchanan became governor.[85]

By 1889 TCI had obtained permission to sublease convicts to other companies, and in 1891 six companies leased more than 700 convicts. When discord erupted in July 1891, the *Nashville Banner* reported that troubles had "been smoldering for many years in the whole mining section of the state."[86] For TCI the convict leasing system, in the words of company vice-president A. S. Colyar, represented "an effective club to hold over the heads of free laborers."[88]

Under the lease provisions TCI obtained the convicts for about 40 cents per day. In return, the Tennessee state government netted more than $770,000 in the two decades between 1870 and 1890, at a time when the annual state budget was about $750,000.[89] So the convict leases contributed about five percent of the state's annual budget.

Even then critics argued that the system was intended to provide cheap labor rather than to rehabilitate criminals. Members of the legislature were aware of the problems. A minority report to an 1889 investigation of the leasing system described the private convict stockades as follows: "These branch prisons are hell holes of rage, cruelty, despair, and vice." They were a "horror and a shame upon the state."[90] Both the Wheel and the Farmers' Alliance took positions opposing the convict-leasing system.[91]

In April 1891 the situation came to a boil when TCI closed a mine for repairs at Briceville, Anderson County, Tennessee. On reopening the mine two months later, the company demanded that wage-earning miners agree to a so-called ironclad contract that rescinded any concessions gained under a contract signed in the prior winter. When miners rejected the contract, the company brought in convict labor.

In the early morning of July 14, 300 miners marched on the convicts' stockade at the mine, demanding surrender of the convicts. The miners then marched the convicts to the train station and sent them to Knoxville. The miners' representatives told the governor they had "come together to defend [their] families from starvation, [their] property from depreciation, and [their] people from contamination from the hands of convict labor."[92]

Governor Buchanan responded by sending three companies of militia to Briceville and going personally to Knoxville to meet with the miners. He invited them to meet him on the evening of July 16. Although he sympathized with the miners, he insisted he would enforce the law:

> *The laws we find on the statute book were made by men elected by you, and it's my business as the executive of the State to see the laws are executed and carried out. . . . while in sympathy with the people suffering, I am equally determined to preserve law and order. . . . The redress of wrongs is not done by mob violence, but by the silent ballot electing men who will give you just laws.*[93]

Eugene Merrell, former miner and then grocery store operator, acted as the miners' spokesman and responded by asking the governor why he did not use the militia to enforce laws violated by the mining companies.

Commissioner of Labor George W. Ford attempted to negotiate a settlement, but the miners refused to yield on the use of convicts. The *Nashville Banner* reported on July 20 that more than 200 miners from Jellico, Tennessee, had arrived in Coal Creek and that many were drunk. Later that day the miners made a second attack with reinforcements from other areas. Some 1,500 miners advanced on the convicts' stockade, whereupon the militia commander surrendered instead of precipitating a violent conflict. This time the miners marched 40 convicts plus their guards and the militia soldiers to the train station and sent them to Knoxville.[94]

Over the next several days, militia units assembled from all over the state until there were as many as 500 troops in Knoxville with more ready to move there. Nationwide attention was now focused on the situation. Samuel Gompers, president of the American Federation of Labor, expressed his sympathy for the miners and criticized the governor.[95] State Attorney General George W. Pickle issued an opinion that the governor did *not* have the authority to declare martial law unless the legislature determined that a state of insurrection existed. But, the opinion continued, the governor had the authority to organize for that possibility.

Buchanan met with the protesters for a second time in Knoxville when the miners presented a formal petition. They demanded "a return to the status quo," annulment of the convict-lease contract, and the calling of a special legislative session to repeal the convict-leasing law. When the company refused to negotiate, the governor felt compelled to enforce the existing law. At that point the situation looked quite dangerous. Despite earlier threats to his own safety made by the miners, Buchanan proposed to march the convicts back to Coal Creek with only the convict guards and no militia escort.[96] Then the miners' resistance collapsed, and a compromise was proposed that called for a 60-day stand-down with the convicts permitted to return but the militia leaving the area. Governor Buchanan promised to call the special legislative session. The *Nashville Banner* on June 25 credited the governor with ending the trouble: "He has averted bloodshed and vindicated the supremacy of the law."[97]

In his call for the special legislative session, Buchanan made 12 requests. His use of the militia at Briceville had been questionable since existing law required the local sheriff to make an explicit request for troops, and the sheriff of Anderson County had telegraphed only "Need Help." Thus the governor asked for legislation to empower the governor to use "force, civil or military, or both" sufficient to execute the laws of the state. He requested the repeal or modification of the laws dealing with the penitentiary and "measures that will reduce the contact and competition of convicts with free labor to the minimum, and conduce at the same time to the humane treatment of the convicts." In accord with the demands of the miners, he asked for laws to prohibit "the use of scrip or its equivalent by persons or corporations in payment of their debts, providing penalty for violation of same, and laws that will punish with penalties any interference with State convicts." He also requested supplementary appropriations to pay for the expenses incurred by the militia in the insurrection and for the special legislative session.[98]

Conflicting interests among Alliance members left the governor's support divided. The legislators voted to approve the governor's "power to repel invasion and suppress insurrections, mobs, or other like unlawful assemblages."[99] They strengthened existing law to prohibit payments in scrip, with criminal penalties for failure to comply. Approved was a bill making it a felony "to make the hindrance, interruption, or interference in any way with the working of convicts, or workhouse prisoners."[100] Provision was made to pay the expenses of the militia for mobilization during the insurrection. A resolution was passed in effect condemning Commissioner of Labor George Ford as being "in a measure responsible for the troubles at Briceville" and encouraging lawlessness.[101] In contrast, the legislators passed a resolution commending Governor Buchanan "for his promptness, energy, firmness, and untiring efforts to restore law and order."[102]

Most important, however, the legislators did *not* change the laws dealing with the convict-leasing system and in effect voted to retain the convict leases. The divisions resulted in the defeat of a resolution that would have pledged the legislature to end convict leasing after the end of the current lease contract. Essentially they abrogated the governor's compromise.[103]

The miners' committee lobbying the legislature during the special session met with the miners on October 28, 1891, reporting the legislature's failure to address the principal concern, namely the convict-leasing system itself. Committee members argued they would be able to accomplish their goals only by electing miners to the legislature. Three nights later miners burned the stockades of the TCI, freed the convicts, provided them clothing, and told them to "go and sin no more."[104] State and county law enforcement agencies were left to search for and recapture these men. As of late November, 150 of the original 450 released convicts remained at large. The *New York Times* quoted the governor as saying it was impossible to identify the men who released the convicts, as they concealed their identity, and the local sentiment in Anderson County favored the miners.[105] Finally in January 1892 the Tennessee Coal, Iron, and Railroad Company compromised and put the free miners back to work at Briceville, moving the convicts to other mines.

The problems with the miners erupted again on August 13, 1892, when TCI laid off the free miners at their mine in Tracy City and brought in convict labor to replace them. After the company rejected the miners' demands, the miners burned the convicts' stockade and put 362 convicts on the train to Nashville. Fifteen convicts escaped, one was killed, and two were recaptured. A situation similar to that in Tracy City occurred at the nearby Inman, Tennessee, convict stockade when miners sent 290 convicts to Nashville and tore down the stockade. On August 15, militia soldiers lynched a miner during a disturbance at a dance in Anderson County. The next day the enraged miners in the Briceville area challenged the militia in their fort, and fighting broke out. Miners from all of the coal producing regions of east Tennessee and Kentucky came to Anderson County to join the fight. Avoiding the strongest military position in Briceville, 1,500 miners attacked the small militia encampment at the Big Mount stockade near Oliver Springs,

Tennessee. After overcoming resistance the miners put 95 convicts and 30 militiamen on a train to Knoxville.

On August 16 the governor ordered troops to move to Oliver Springs. He also stated that he was going to the scene himself and announced his determination to end the crisis:

> *I shall declare the lease void. Why? Because the other branch prisons have been wiped out and the lessees have refused to have anything to do with the convicts. Every political party is against the lease, and I believe that the people are against it. It may be called cowardly and illegal, but it is the only thing that can be done now. I am doing my best to keep the miners up there quiet until I can get there.*[106]

Despite efforts to quiet the situation, the violence continued. At that point the governor sent 500 troops to Anderson County, and about an equal number of miners were arrested. Unfortunately some miners continued to fight, with the result that 27 deaths occurred. Strike leader D. B. Monroe was arrested, convicted, and sentenced to prison for seven years, of which he served two.[107]

The public directed the major share of its outrage for the entire affair at Governor Buchanan. Historian Roger Hart concludes:

> *Governor Buchanan was hurt by a crisis not of his own making. He was caught between businessmen who considered the strike 'a crime without parallel' and laws he felt duty-bound to enforce, on the one hand, and, on the other, the strong feeling of labor and reformers that the*

lease system was a disgraceful injustice. . . . Although it is hard to imagine how he could have been more fair, the feebleness of Buchanan's official powers and the paucity of his political experience made him vulnerable to the enemies of the Alliance."[108]

With the election of 1892 only weeks away, the turmoil dealt a severe blow to Buchanan's hopes for reelection.

In his final address to the legislature, Governor Buchanan recommended that the state build a new penitentiary to provide a place to house the convict population abandoned by the private lessees. The hard lessons of the previous two years were taken to heart, and on March 25, 1893, a bill passed the new legislature "to prepare for the abolition of the convict lease system." It provided for the construction of a new prison facility, eventually built at Brushy Mountain, which operated until 2009. The leasing companies abandoned the leases in 1893 even before they expired in 1896.[109]

THE GUBERNATORIAL ELECTION OF 1892

Almost as soon as the election of 1890 concluded, the establishment Bourbon Democrats had begun to plan the recapture of the governor's chair. From the outset of the Buchanan administration, the critics readied their knives and challenged Buchanan at every opportunity. Historian Roger Hart writes, "The losers of 1890 were not going to underestimate the Alliance again, nor did they intend to divide and weaken their forces a second time."[110]

Once again many important Democratic newspapers opposed Buchanan's reelection. By early 1892 the old Democratic hierarchy settled on Peter Turney, Chief Justice of the Tennessee Supreme Court, as their candidate and leader. Through the early spring of 1892, Turney and Buchanan supporters battled in county primaries and conventions, with Buchanan successfully regaining the number of delegates he had earned in 1890.[111]

One issue dividing Democrats in 1892 was the subtreasury land and loan scheme, which Alliancemen favored as an answer to the problems of financing farm operations and which, in effect, supported farm prices. The premise of the subtreasury plan was to permit farmers to use their nonperishable crops as collateral for government loans at subsidized interest rates. Farmers could store their crops in government warehouses until prices reached attractive levels.[112] Critics argued that the plan was discriminatory, benefiting the few at the general taxpayers' expense.[113] Opponents again tried to paint the Alliancemen as members of a secret order intending to gain advantage over nonfarmers, but Tennessee Alliance members were quite conservative. At the southern Alliance meeting in Ocala, Florida, in December 1890, only one of three delegates including John Price Buchanan voted for the plan, while the convention voted nearly eight to one for it.[114]

Though they differed over the subtreasury issue, the main point of contention between the Alliance and the establishment Bourbons was control of the party. When the Buchanan campaign showed signs of having considerable strength at the state Democratic convention, the Turney forces proposed changes in the nominating process. First they called for eliminating stump speeches, a traditional part of electioneering during the period. Second, they proposed that only persons who renounced the subtreasury plan be admitted to vote in Democratic primaries and conventions.[115]

Despite the calls to abstain from stump speeches, some old-line Democrats took to the stump to denounce the Alliance and, by implication, Buchanan. Former governor Bob Taylor declared the election a fight for the life of the Democratic Party. Buchanan's 1890 opponent Josiah Patterson described Alliance leaders as "the most arrogant set of knaves that ever masqueraded in any political guise or any so-called set of principles."[116]

Buchanan's campaign for renomination showed early strength before the state Democratic convention, but his support dwindled as the convention approached. As a result, Buchanan withdrew his name from consideration for the Democratic nomination on July 30.[117]

Buchanan's longtime advocate J. H. McDowell went on record as saying the governor had "been defrauded out of the nomination."[118] A group of Buchanan supporters urged him to pursue his candidacy as an independent:

Dear Sir: We, the undersigned, having observed the unmanly, undemocratic and proscriptive policy of the friends of Judge Turney, resulting in your declination to go before the state convention as a candidate for Governor, do respectfully and earnestly beg you to recall your determination to retire from the contest, and to announce yourself as an independent candidate for Governor.[119]

The August 9 Democratic convention adopted the rule that primary voters and convention delegates had to swear an oath rejecting the subtreasury plan.[120] This rule shut Alliancemen and Buchanan supporters out of the proceedings. Turney was nominated on the first ballot. Buchanan garnered only a few votes. After the convention some groups of delegates stated that they were friends of John P. Buchanan but loyal Democrats first and could not support any independent candidacy on his part.[121]

On August 15 Buchanan announced his candidacy as an "independent Jeffersonian Democrat." His insistence on preserving a connection with the Democratic Party is consistent with his position in 1890 and his rejection of a third-party nomination in 1892. He contended that "thousands of voters" demanded he stand for reelection.[122] His platform included a call for the direct election of U.S. Senators, free trade, limitation of trading in agricultural futures, a graduated income tax, an end to the convict-leasing system, legal provision for the arbitration of strikes, child-labor legislation, and support for public schools.

While the Democrats worked to push the Alliancemen out, a new political group styled the People's Party, or simply the Populists, tried to entice them to join. In June 1892 Alliance leader and Buchanan mentor John H. McDowell reluctantly, in his words, abandoned the Democrats and joined the People's Party.[123] Buchanan immediately announced his opposition to a third party and issued a public statement on his position: "I am opposed to a third party or people's party." He knew that many of his followers were loyal to the Democratic Party and would not abandon their allegiance.[124]

The People's Party held its convention in Nashville in mid-August and voted to support Buchanan. There was a resolution to appoint a committee to meet "with any other party" to consider a joint slate of congressional and state-level candidates, the presumption being that the other party would be the Republicans. As events developed Buchanan supporters were forced to declare either for the Populists or for Turney.[125]

A final blow to the Buchanan campaign came as a result of a scandal precipitated by others. The *Knoxville Journal*, never a Buchanan supporter, printed letters among Republicans detailing an agreement between the National Republican Party and John H. McDowell. The paper charged they had agreed that for $15,000 in campaign funds, McDowell would endeavor to keep Buchanan in the governor's race, with the hope that the Republican candidate G. W. Winstead would benefit. The money would go to support Populist candidates and the Buchanan campaign. The exposure on October 23, 1892, of this agreement seriously damaged the Populists' efforts and tarred Buchanan.[126]

In the general election Turney won the governor's race with 126,348 votes, or 48.8 percent, compared to 100,577 votes, or 38.9 percent, for Winstead, and 31,512 votes, or 12.2 percent, for Buchanan.[127] In other words, the Democratic candidate lost votes relative to the 1890 race, the Republican gained slightly, and the independent candidate more than doubled his share of the 1890 vote. Historian Connie Lester argues that the farm voters still challenged the Bourbons and the New South establishment.[128]

In the congressional races Republicans won their usual seats in east Tennessee, while Democrats won the other eight seats including the strongly contested third district. The Populists ran strongly in seven of the eight middle and west Tennessee districts. Only in Memphis, the 10th district, did the Democratic candidate win handily. The People's Party elected only five to the General Assembly and one to the Senate, down from 54 Alliancemen in the 1891–1893 legislature.[129]

THE LEGACY OF JOHN PRICE BUCHANAN

John Price Buchanan's role as a public officeholder had ended, but his involvement in Tennessee politics did not. In 1894 the former governor attended the state Populist convention, where he continued to have supporters, but he never declared himself a Populist, preferring to retain his own Independent Democrat label. After that convention Buchanan was sued in his role as a board member of the *Farmers' Voice*. The plaintiff in the suit, the paper's editor and an ally of John H. McDowell, complained that Buchanan had tried to exert undue influence on the paper's editorial positions. Buchanan responded by complaining the paper gave too much support to the People's Party, indicating his own political preference.

Further evidence of his continuing interest in the issues that sparked his political involvement came in June 1895, when a convention of supporters of bimetallism met in Memphis. Bimetallism refers to a monetary system in which two metals, gold and silver, serve as the currency standard. This system had been used by the United States until 1873, when the country switched to the single gold standard. A return to bimetallism became a major issue for Populists of all stripes as a means of inflating the currency. More than 2,200 delegates, Democrats, Republicans, and Populists, from 21 states attended the convention. They included such old enemies as Bourbons, New South Democrats, Alliancemen, and John Price Buchanan.[130]

The former governor returned to the Democratic fold completely by the early 20th century. Connie Lester argues that his agrarian views still resonated with Tennessee voters. As a result Buchanan frequently appeared as the elder statesman with Democratic office seekers.[131]

During his two years as governor, his wife Fannie had visited Nashville as much as she could, at a time when there was no official governor's residence.[132] Instead she remained at home to manage the farm and their eight children. The governor's grandson, the Nobel Laureate, recounted the story that his father, James M. Buchanan, told about his father, John Price Buchanan. Long after his term as governor, in order to maintain a presence in Tennessee politics, John Price Buchanan regularly took the train to Nashville from Murfreesboro and returned in the evening to the farm. The young Jim Buchanan would drive a wagon to the train station to pick up his father for the return home.[133] The former governor also participated in agricultural institutes sponsored by the Commissioner of Agriculture in the precursor to the agricultural extension service of the University of Tennessee.[134] Though he may have been out of elective office, John Price Buchanan was not finished with public affairs.

Some have dismissed John Price Buchanan's brief political career as a fluke, the story of a common man who achieved the governorship by shear happenstance. However, here was a man who started on his own as a teenager in a new community. By his own initiative he built a successful farming business during a challenging time. His neighbors thought enough of him to elect him to the state legislature twice. He inspired enough people across the state of Tennessee to choose him to represent their views about the vexing problems facing farmers. Through his own perseverance and character, he put himself in the position to be a legitimate candidate for governor of Tennessee and for a season overcame the daunting opposition of the Democratic Party establishment. As governor he faced challenges created long before his time in office and was commended for his ability to deal with them. Those qualities can hardly be ascribed to a man who reached his station by mere luck.

By the time Buchanan assumed the office, Tennessee's Bourbon politicians were determined to recapture control of the governorship. They commanded substantial skill and experience, which they cunningly employed in the legislature and in nominating conventions. Four years earlier they had very nearly denied renomination to a popular governor, Bob Taylor, who repeatedly demonstrated his great appeal to voters.

Ultimately many of the positions for which Buchanan campaigned became enacted into law. The convict-leasing system was ended in 1896. In 1899 the state of Tennessee required each county to provide facilities for secondary education. The 16th Amendment to the U.S. Constitution imposed a federal income tax in 1913; in the same year the 17th Amendment provided for the direct election of members of the Senate. Federal law supporting arbitration of labor disputes was passed in 1925. The "Fair Labor Standards Act" of 1938 finally produced federal law regulating child labor. Advocacy of free trade became the stated policy of the U.S. in 1947 with the creation of the International Trade Organization, which preceded the General Agreement on Tariffs and Trade. While John Price Buchanan cannot be credited with the fulfillment of those positions that he advocated, he can be recognized as a man of vision and foresight.

There are both parallels and contrasts between the politician John Price Buchanan and his grandson, the political economist James McGill Buchanan Jr. In the first case, both can be said to have raised themselves by their bootstraps from fairly modest beginnings to positions of respect among their peers. They achieved that respect by their own hard work and resilience in the face of substantial obstacles. On the other hand, they did not see the world through exactly the same lens. One was a man of the soil, while the other was an intellectual. Many of the ideas John Price espoused his grandson would oppose. Those very policies associated with the governor in the previous paragraph would likely not appeal to the Nobel Prize–winning economist. Whereas the grandfather advocated what might be termed interventionist public policies, the libertarian grandson would find many of those ideas objectionable. The latter's views will be explored in more detail in a later chapter.

Notes

1. The earliest surviving tax records for Rutherford County date from 1877 and indicate that John P. Buchanan paid taxes on two parcels of land totaling 219 acres and valued at $2,500. The largest plot was 185 acres in the south end of the county along the Manchester Pike. Rutherford County Tax Records, 1877–1878 (Tax Duplicates, Rutherford County Archives). Carol Hoffman, *Rutherford County Historical Society Publication*, No. 21 (Summer 1983), p. 65.

2. There have been a number of attempts to estimate the cost of the war for the country in terms of its effect on economic growth in the post-war South, and the difficulties in making accurate estimates are many. Claudia Golden and Frank D. Lewis, "The Economic Cost of the American Civil War: Estimates and Implications," *Journal of Economic History*, Vol. 35, No. 2 (June 1975), pp. 299–326. Roger Ransom and Richard Sutch, "The Impact of the Civil War and Emancipation on Southern Agriculture," *Explorations in Economic History*, Vol. 12 (1975), pp. 1–28. Peter Temin, "The Post-Bellum Recovery of the South and the Cost of the Civil War," *Journal of Economic History*, Vol. 36, No. 42 (Dec. 1976), pp. 898–907. Gavin Wright, "Cotton Competition and the Post-Bellum Recovery of the American South," *Journal of Economic History*, Vol. 34, No. 3 (Sept. 1974), pp. 610–635.

3. Robert Tracy McKenzie, *One South or Many? Plantation Belt and Upcountry in Civil War–Era Tennessee* (New York: Cambridge University Press, 2002), p. 97–98.

4. "Historical Statistics of the United States 1789–1945, a Supplement to the Statistical Abstract of the United States,"

http://www2.census.gov/prod2/statcomp/documents/Historical StatisticsoftheUnitedStates1789-1945.pdf, retrieved March 15, 2011.

5. "In fact as late as 1909, Southerners on average consumed roughly thirty percent less than had per capita consumption continued to grow after 1860 at the antebellum rate." Golden and Lewis, "The Economic Cost of the American Civil War," p. 319.

6. Temin, "The Post-Bellum Recovery of the South," p. 907. The impact of the end of slavery on the recovery of the South is also found in Roger Ransom and Richard Sutch, "The Impact of the Civil War and Emancipation on Southern Agriculture," *Explorations in Economic History* 12 (1975), pp. 1–28.

7. Economists continue to debate whether technological innovation forced farmers and farm labor to leave the farm or whether they were induced to leave by more attractive alternatives in urban areas. For an argument supporting the latter, see Colin Thirtle, David Schimmelpfennig, and Robert F. Townsend, "Induced Innovation in United States Agriculture, 1880–1990: Time Series Tests and an Error Correction Model," *American Journal of Agricultural Economics*, Vol. 84 (August 2002), pp. 598–614.

8. U.S. Census 1870, "Productions of Agriculture," p. 81, and U.S. Census 1880, "Statistics of Agriculture," p. 3.

9. U.S. Census 1870, "Persons Engaged in Each Occupation," Table, XXVII, p. 675; U.S. Census 1880, "Occupations," Table XXIX, p. 712; U.S. Census 1890, "Statistics of Population," Table 1, p. 30.

10. A complete record of business cycles of the U.S. economy

is maintained by the National Bureau of Economic Research (NBER), *http://www.nber.org/cycles/cyclesmain.html*, retrieved September 24, 2007. For a discussion of the impact of the depression of 1873, see also O. V. Wells, "The Depression of 1873–79," *Journal of Farm Economics*, Vol. 19, No. 2 (May 1937), pp. 621–633.

11. Connie L. Lester, *Up from the Mudsills of Hell: The Farmers' Alliance, Populism, and Progressive Agriculture in Tennessee, 1870–1915* (Athens, GA: University of Georgia Press, 2006), p. 23.

12. When McKenzie modifies the per-farm values for the decline in farm size by measuring median value of production per acre, there is no decline in the value of production per acre. That would have been of little comfort to the farm families of the period. McKenzie, *One South or Many?*, pp. 184–185.

13. Ibid., pp. 186–187.

14. Louis M. Kyriakoudes, *The Social Origins of the Urban South: Race, Gender, and Migration in Nashville and Middle Tennessee, 1890–1930* (Chapel Hill, NC: University of North Carolina Press, 2003), p. 40; David B. Grigg, *Population Growth and Agrarian Change: An Historical Perspective* (Cambridge, England: Cambridge University Press, 1980), pp. 25–26.

15. Rutherford County Tax Records, 1877–1878 (Tax Duplicates, Rutherford County Archives).

16. Anne Mayhew, "A Reappraisal of the Causes of Farm Protest in the United States, 1870–1900," *Journal of Economic History*, Vol. 32, No. 2 (June 1972), pp. 464–475.

17. Ibid., p. 469. For a similar argument see William J. Cooper Jr. and Thomas E. Terrill, *The American South: A History*, 2nd ed. (New York: McGraw-Hill, 1996), pp. 490–491.

18. Lester, *Up from the Mudsills of Hell*, p. 40.

19 Roger L. Hart, *Redeemers, Bourbons, and Populists: Tennessee, 1870–1896*, (Baton Rouge, LA: Louisiana State University Press, 1975), pp. 229–230.

20. McKenzie, *One South or Many?*, pp. 35–38.

21. Ibid., p. 188. McKenzie leaves the reader with a warning that his methodology, that of examining a sample of communities rather than a canvas of all, leaves open the possibility of gaining a mistaken view of the times (pp. 190–195).

22. Agricultural societies appeared as early as 1819 in the form of the Cumberland Agricultural Society in Davidson County. They were primarily a forum for discussion of farming techniques and in the 1840s became sponsors of county fairs. The disruptions brought on by the Civil War resulted in the disappearance of these organizations. Donald L. Winters, "Agricultural Societies," *Tennessee Encyclopedia of History and Culture*, *http://tennesseeencyclopedia.net/imagegallery.php?EntryID=A010*, retrieved July 19, 2012. In 1869, Oliver H. Kelley and six other members of the U.S. Department of Agriculture founded the Order of the Patrons of Husbandry. Better known as the Grange, it was a fraternal organization with the aim of improving the economic and social condition of the farming community. The National Grange continues today (*http://www.nationalgrange.org/about/history.html*, retrieved July 19, 2012). Initially the growth of the organization was slow, but sparked by the Panic of 1873 member-

ship grew rapidly. Membership in the Grange peaked in Tennessee with 19,780 families in 1875 and fell just as rapidly to 1,474 by 1877 and no members by 1880. This organization was primarily a social entity and did not advocate political actions. It was unique in that the Grange welcomed women members as well as men. Hart, *Redeemers, Bourbons, and Populists*, p. 111.

23. The Wheel philosophy was that economic problems occurred due to a divergence from *natural law*. Wheel historian W. Scott Morgan observed that "man is naturally disposed to take pleasure in remunerative employment . . . [and] is justly entitled to the fruits of his own labor. . . . Any violation of this natural law will breed social disorder." Monopoly power perverted the natural order, he believed, but this could be remedied by political action. Lester, *Up from the Mudsills of Hell*, pp. 58–59, 60–61.

24. Source: *http://www.anythingarkansas.com/arkapedia/pedia/ Agricultural_Wheel*, retrieved July 19, 2012.

25. Lester, *Up from the Mudsills of Hell*, p. 61.

27. Ibid., p. 62; Donna A. Barnes, "Farmers' Alliance," *The Handbook of Texas Online*, *http://www.tsha.utexas.edu/handbook/ online/articles/FF/aaf2.html*, retrieved July 9, 2007.

28. Lester, *Up from the Mudsills of Hell*, p. 100.

29. Farmer cooperatives were a popular idea of the 1880s and later, but goodwill and good intentions were not enough to make them successful. Reluctance on the part of farmer members to commit to the co-op by providing necessary capital for operations and, perhaps more important, competition from existing business made survival difficult for many co-ops.

30. "A Big Boycott Proposed," *New York Times*, August 13, 1890, p. 1 (*New York Times* Archive).

31. Ibid., pp. 109–116.

32. A decade earlier the issue of taxing to pay for debt service had became a concern of farmers. Much of the $39 million state debt as of 1869 was due to railroad construction and to debt incurred by the post–Civil War Brownlow administration. Facing hard times, farmers were resentful of paying taxes to service debt held by "rich" bondholders and suspicious of corruption during the Brownlow years. During the 1870s and 1880s, the issue continued to resonate with various proposals to pay off the debt. Hart, *Redeemers, Bourbons, and Populists*, p. 19.

33. Hart, *Redeemers, Bourbons, and Populists*, pp. 52–53. Two years later the legislature passed a law refunding the debt at 50 cents on the dollar. It proved a permanent solution. Robert B. Jones III, *Tennessee at the Crossroads: The State Debt Controversy, 1870–1883* (Knoxville, TN: University of Tennessee, 1977).

34. *Biographical Directory, Tennessee General Assembly, 1796–1967* (Preliminary, No. 6), Rutherford County.

35. Carol Hoffman, "John Price Buchanan, Farmer and Politician," *Rutherford County Historical Society Publication*, No. 21 (Summer 1983), pp. 70–71.

36. Hart, *Redeemers, Bourbons, and Populists*, p. 123.

37. Connie Lester, "Farmers' Alliance," *Tennessee Encyclopedia of History and Culture, http://tennesseeencyclopedia.net*, retrieved August 8, 2007.

38. Hart, *Redeemers, Bourbons, and Populists*, p. 113.

39. Ibid., pp. 113–114.

40. Lester, *Up from the Mudsills of Hell*, p. 94.

41. Cooper and Terrill, *The American South*, pp. 432–434.

42. When faced with a choice of supporting Alliance candidates, many farmers could not abandon the Democratic candidate. I am indebted to Dr. Connie Lester for clarifying this paradox of the allegiance to the Confederate cause and the Democratic Party for Alliancemen.

43. Although most historians have portrayed the poll tax as a measure to disenfranchise African Americans, John McDowell, publisher of the *Weekly Toiler*, the voice of the Farmers' Alliance, argued that the poll tax was a means of funding public education. Lester concludes that "For Alliancemen, the poll tax offered two potential benefits: the assurance of white, Democratic rule and a mechanism for increasing the school fund that did not fall disproportionately on the farmers of the state." Lester, *Up from the Mudsills of Hell*, pp. 140–141.

44. Connie Lester, "*Disfranchising Laws*," *Tennessee Encyclopedia of History and Culture*, http://tennesseeencyclopedia.net/, retrieved July 17, 2007; Lester, *Up from the Mudsills of Hell*, p. 139. Margaret Endsley Holloway, *The Reaction in Tennessee to the Federal Elections Bill of 1890* (M.A. Thesis, University of Tennessee, December 1970); *Tennessee Blue Book*, http://state.tn.us/sos/bluebook/05-06/43-past_cons.pdf.

45. Jimmie Lewis Franklin, "Civil Rights Movement,"

Tennessee Encyclopedia of History and Culture, http://tennesseeencyclopedia.net/entry.php?rec=264, retrieved July 19, 2012.

46. Hart, *Redeemers, Bourbons, and Populists*, pp. 6–7.

47. Ibid., p. 131.

48. Lester, *Up from the Mudsills of Hell*, pp. 100–101; Hoffman, "John Price Buchanan," pp. 70–71.

49. Lester, *Up from the Mudsills of Hell*, p. 160.

50. Ibid., pp. 160–161.

51. Ibid., p. 161.

52. Hart, *Redeemers, Bourbons, and Populists*, p. 138.

53. Ibid., p. 138.

54. "Buchanan Still Leads," *New York Times*, July 18, 1890, p. 5 (*New York Times* Archive).

55. Lester, *Up from the Mudsills of Hell*, p, 163.

56. Hart, *Redeemers, Bourbons, and Populists*, p. 146.

57. Hoffman, "John Price Buchanan," p. 74.

58. Ibid., p. 75.

59. Lester, *Up from the Mudsills of Hell*, p. 168.

60. Hart, *Redeemers, Bourbons, and Populists*, p. 148.

61. Hart, *Redeemers, Bourbons, and Populists*, p. 147.

62. Lewis Baxter, Republican, was not related to Jere Baxter, Democrat.

63. Ibid., pp. 152–153. Holloway, *The Reaction in Tennessee to the Federal Elections Bill of 1890*, pp. 31–33.

64. Hoffman, "John Price Buchanan," p. 78.

65. The congressional candidates supported by the Alliance were elected in Tennessee, contributing to a new Democratic majority in the U.S. Congress in the 1890 election. Lester, *Up from the Mudsills of Hell*, p. 169.

66. Hoffman, "John Price Buchanan," pp. 78–79; Lester, *Up from the Mudsills of Hell*, p. 96.

67. Lester, *Up from the Mudsills of Hell*, p. 170.

68. Hart, *Redeemers, Bourbons, and Populists*, p. 158.

69. Ibid., p. 178.

70. Tennessee farmers had urged the U.S. Congress to create a federal Department of Agriculture and to instruct U.S. legates abroad to promote American agricultural exports. Hart, *Redeemers, Bourbons, and Populists*, pp. 180–189; Lester, *Up from the Mudsills of Hell*, pp. 142–149.

71. Lester, *Up from the Mudsills of Hell*, pp. 142–146, 177.

72. Bourbon Democrats of Tennessee were the most conservative and resistant to change. They had supported railroad regulation in 1883. In the conservative Bourbon view, railroads were agents of change, subject to corruption, and exploiters of farmers.

73. Hart, *Redeemers, Bourbons, and Populists*, pp. 72–73. In fact, railroad rates have always been quite complicated with different shippers paying different tariffs. They continued thus through the era of railroad regulation from 1887 through the 1970s. Furthermore, other transportation modes exhibit similar pricing behavior even today. Economists contend that such pricing is necessary to encourage the offering of those transportation services to the greatest extent possible.

74. Ibid., pp. 74, 93.

75. Lester, *Up from the Mudsills of Hell*, p. 153; Hart, *Redeemers, Bourbons, and Populists*, p. 158.

76. Lester, *Up from the Mudsills of Hell*, p. 172.

77. Ibid., p. 172.

78. Ibid., p. 173.

79. *Governor's Address*, 1891, p. 15.

80. Ibid., pp. 16–17.

81. Lester, *Up from the Mudsills of Hell*, p. 177.

82. Ibid., p. 177.

83. Some of the works that focus on the industrialization and coal mining of the New South include Ronald D. Eller, *Miners, Millhands, and Mountaineers: Industrialization of the Appalachian South, 1880–1930* (Knoxville, TN: University of Tennessee Press, 1982); Crandall A. Shiflett, *Coal Towns: Life, Work, and Culture in the Company Towns of Southern Appalachia, 1880–1960* (Knoxville, TN: University of Tennessee Press, 1991); Karin A. Shapiro, *A New South Rebellion: The Battle Against Convict Labor in the Tennessee Coalfields, 1871–1986* (Chapel Hill, NC: University of North Carolina Press, 1998).

84. For the offense of stealing as little as eight cents' worth of fence rails, men were imprisoned. In retrospect, it can be charged that Tennessee state laws regarding trespass and vagrancy were aimed at controlling black labor. John B. Jones Jr., "Convict Lease Wars," *Tennessee Encyclopedia of History and Culture*, *http://tennesseeencyclopedia.net*, retrieved July 12, 2007; *Lester, Up from the Mudsills of Hell*, p. 174; Matthew J. Mancini, *One Dies, Get Another, Convict Leasing in the American South, 1866–1928*, (Columbia, SC: University of South Carolina Press, 1996), pp. 2–3.

85. James B. Jones Jr., "Convict Leasing Wars," *http://tennesseeencyclopedia.net/entry.php?rec=306*, retrieved July 19, 2012.

86. *Nashville Banner*, Vol. XVI, No. 82 (July 16, 1891), p. 1 (Tennessee State Library and Archives).

88. Among the convicts about 75 percent were black as compared with only six percent of the free miners. Racist attitudes of

the era only would have added fuel to the fire. Pete Daniel, "The Tennessee Convict War," *Tennessee Historical Quarterly*, (Fall 1975), p. 274; John B. Jones Jr., "Convict Lease Wars."

89. "Appropriations Bill," *Acts of Tennessee 1889* (Nashville, TN: Marshall & Bruce, 1889).

90. Mancini, *One Dies, Get Another*, p. 160.

91. Hart, *Redeemers, Bourbons, and Populists*, p. 172; Jones, p. 204; Lester, *Up from the Mudsills of Hell*, p. 174.

92. Lester, *Up from the Mudsills of Hell*, pp. 174–175.

93. *Nashville Banner*, Vol. XVI, No. 84 (July 18, 1891), p. 1 (Tennessee State Library and Archives).

94. Daniel, "The Tennessee Convict War," pp. 276–278; Lester, *Up from the Mudsills of Hell*, pp. 174–175.

95. *Nashville Banner*, Vol. XVI, No. 86 (July 21, 1891), p. 1, No. 87 (July 22, 1891) p. 1 (Tennessee State Library and Archives).

96. *Nashville Banner*, Vol. XVI, No. 89, (July 24, 1891), p. 1 (Tennessee State Library and Archives).

97. *Nashville Banner*, Vol. XVI, No. 90 (July 25, 1891), p. 1 (Tennessee State Library and Archives).

98. In keeping with his view on the efficient use of the legislature's time and taxpayer expense, he asked for consideration of several matters that did not pertain to the miners' strike. For example, he requested some redistricting of state and congressio-

nal districts, changes in the circuit and chancery court divisions, and an appropriation to pay for a Tennessee exhibit at the Chicago World's Columbian Exposition. "Proclamation," *Public Acts of Extraordinary Session, 1891* (Supplemental Volume), pp. 7–9.

99. Ibid., pp. 22–23.

100. Ibid., pp. 31–32.

101. Ibid., Joint House Resolution 16, pp. 104–105.

102. *Public Acts of Extraordinary Session, 1891* (Supplemental Volume) Senate Resolution 2.

103. As for the other matters considered, the legislature passed a bill to prohibit prizefighting among other things. Ibid., pp. 18–33.

104. Daniel, "The Tennessee Convict War," p. 285.

105. "Governor Buchanan Talks," *New York Times*, December 11, 1891, p. 2. (*New York Times* Archives).

106. *Nashville Banner*, Vol. XVII, No. 114 (August 16, 1892), p. 1 (Tennessee State Library and Archives).

107. Daniel, "The Tennessee Convict War," pp. 288–292; Hart, *Redeemers, Bourbons, and Populists*, p. 192; Lester, *Up from the Mudsills of Hell*, pp. 191–192.

108. Hart, *Redeemers, Bourbons, and Populists*, p. 175.

109. Mancini, *One Dies, Get Another*, pp. 165–166; *http://www. tennessee.gov/correction/institutions/mccx.html*, retrieved March

15, 2011.

110. Hart, *Redeemers, Bourbons, and Populists*, p. 178.

111. Ibid., pp. 178–180, 181; Lester, *Up from the Mudsills of Hell*, pp. 178–179.

112. Cooper and Terrill, *The American South*, pp. 500–501. "Subtreasury Land and Loan System," *U.S. History Companion*, Houghton Mifflin Company, *www.answers.com*, retrieved July 12, 2007.

113. Lester, *Up from the Mudsills of Hell*, p. 182. The Bourbons tried to make that connection with railroad interests, another target of Alliance hostility, one notable example being Leland Stanford, railroad tycoon and president of the Central Pacific Railroad.

114. Hart, *Redeemers, Bourbons, and Populists*, p. 168.

115. Ibid., p. 184.

116. Ibid., p. 186.

117. Hart, *Redeemers, Bourbons, and Populists*, p. 190.

118. *Nashville Banner*, Vol. XVII, No. 101 (August 1, 1892), p. 1 (Tennessee State Library and Archives).

119. *Nashville Banner*, Vol. XVII, No. 106 (August 6, 1892), p. 1 (Tennessee State Library and Archives).

120. Although the subtreasury plan was rejected by Tennessee Democrats and the U.S. Congress in its original form, by the

1920s Congress had approved two price-fixing measures, and in 1933 even before the new Roosevelt Administration was in place, Congress passed the Agricultural Adjustment Act. That act shared a number of features with the subtreasury plan. John Mark Hansen, *Gaining Access: Congress and the Farm Lobby, 1919–1981* (Chicago: University of Chicago Press, 1991), pp. 26, 75.

121. *Nashville Banner*, Vol. XVII, No. 107 (August 10, 1892), p. 1; Vol. XVII, No. 114 (August 16, 1892), p. 2 (Tennessee State Library and Archives).

122. *Nashville Banner*, Vol. XVII, No. 113 (August 15, 1892), p. 1 (Tennessee State Library and Archives).

123. Lester, *Up from the Mudsills of Hell*, p. 189.

124. Hart contends that the People's Party of Tennessee was founded by members of the Union Labor Party, which had received a total of 48 votes in the 1890 presidential election. Hart, *Redeemers, Bourbons, and Populists*, pp. 184, 188.

125. For president they endorsed the People's Party candidates James B. Weaver and James B. Field. Weaver had been a general in the Union Army, while Field served in the Confederate Army. Lester, *Up from the Mudsills of Hell*, p. 190; Hart, *Redeemers, Bourbons, and Populists*, pp. 186–187.

126. Lester, *Up from the Mudsills of Hell*, pp. 193–194.

127. Turney remained as chief justice until he was inaugurated. This maneuver enabled him to appoint his successor. See James W. Ely Jr, ed., *A History of the Tennessee Supreme Court* (Knoxville, TN: University of Tennessee Press, 2002), pp. 154–157.

128. Ibid., p. 196. Peter Turney was inaugurated January 16, 1893.

129. Ibid., pp. 195–196.

130. Ibid., p. 202.

131. Lester, *Up from the Mudsills of Hell*, pp. 206–207.

132. Margaret I. Phillips, *The Governors of Tennessee* (Gretna, LA: Pelican Publishing Company, 1978), p. 109. Phillips notes, p. 122, that Tennessee did not appropriate money for a governor's mansion until 1907.

133. Interview with James M. Buchanan Jr., May 16, 2007, Indianapolis, IN.

134. Ibid., pp. 210–211.

CHAPTER VI.

THE BUCHANAN FAMILY IN THE 20TH CENTURY

JAMES SHANNON BUCHANAN

While in the 19th century the Buchanan family was distinguished for its leadership in the community and the political world, the 20th century Buchanans distinguished themselves in educational and intellectual endeavors. As early as Major John Buchanan's authoring of his *Arithmetic*, the family evidenced an interest in education beyond that of most of their neighbors. Thomas Buchanan and both of his sons had attended secondary school, something relatively rare for farm children in the mid-1800s. Even though John Price Buchanan did not attend college, his interest in economic affairs and participation in agricultural institutes indicate a curious mind and an education in the school of life. However, this next generation of Buchanans would far surpass their parents and grandparents' educational achievements.

James Shannon Buchanan, the third child of Thomas and Rebecca Jane Buchanan, was born October 14, 1864,

Figure 11. James Shannon Buchanan, University of Oklahoma

when his older brother, John Price Buchanan, was fighting with Roddy's Escort Cavalry Regiment. Like his brother, he was educated in the community schools and the Harpeth Academy in Franklin, Tennessee. However, unlike his sibling he continued his education about 30 miles east of

Nashville in Lebanon, Tennessee, at Cumberland University, founded in 1842 by the Cumberland Presbyterian Church.[1] It is quite likely that he would have had at least one class under Andrew Hays Buchanan (1828–1914), who taught mathematics there and whose connection to the Buchanan family of interest here is unknown but possible.[2] James graduated in 1885 with a Bachelor of Science degree.

After graduating, James Shannon Buchanan served as principal of the Cornersville Institute, an elementary school in Cornersville, Tennessee, from 1886 to 1889.[3] In 1890 he became the clerk, or assistant superintendent, of public schools of the State of Tennessee. In that position he earned the princely sum of $1,000 per year, compared with a national average teacher's salary of $256 in 1890, and supplemented his income by lecturing at the Watkins Institute of Nashville.[4] Also, he did graduate work at Vanderbilt University in 1893–1894. In 1894 he moved to Edmond, Oklahoma Territory, and joined the faculty of the two-year-old Central Normal School, now the University of Central Oklahoma.[5]

The next year, 1895, James S. Buchanan moved to the University of Oklahoma as a professor of history. In that first year, he and Mary J. Overstreet, the first female faculty member at the university, served on a selection committee that chose the new institution's colors, red and "corn."[6] In 1896 he did further graduate study at the University of Chicago. Later, reflecting the university's development, he became the first dean of the College of Arts and Sciences in 1908.

James received his final academic credential, an honorary Doctor of Laws, or LL.D. degree, from Kingfisher

Figure 12. Panoramic view, Kingfisher College

College in 1917. The Congregationalist Church founded the college in 1890 in Kingfisher, Oklahoma. Following the closure of Kingfisher College in 1927, the contents of the college library went to the University of Oklahoma under the terms of an agreement between the two institutions. In return the university administered the records of Kingfisher graduates. Today the Kingfisher College name is honored by the Kingfisher College Professor of Philosophy in the Department of Philosophy at the university.[7]

In 1923 the university president was dismissed, and Dr. Buchanan was appointed acting president of the institution. He was awarded the title of president in 1924 and served in that capacity until 1925.[8] At that point he assumed the position of vice president and held that post until he died in 1930. A colleague remembered him with affection:

He was plain spoken, sometimes almost to bluntness. An amused smile, a sarcastic speech, or a hostile grunt, was his usual answer to a pretentious display of knowledge or to an exhibition of bad taste of any kind.[9]

Like his brother, James maintained a love of politics. His only elective experiences were on the Norman City Council and in 1906–1907 as a member of the Oklahoma Constitutional Convention. He described the constitutional process in some detail in his own history of the state. Under the provision of the Enabling Act signed by President Theodore Roosevelt in June 1906, 55 members of the convention were elected, from both the Oklahoma and Indian territories with an additional two from the Osage Indian Reservation, to prepare for the creation of the state of Oklahoma.[10] James Buchanan was one of those elected from the Oklahoma Territory.[11] Here is another instance, like that of the Cumberland Compact, of a concurrence of events relating to the writing of a constitutional document and the Buchanan family. As will be discussed below, the role of constitutions as a framework for governance is a significant part of the research of Nobel Prize winner James M. Buchanan.

Oklahoma students adopted the name Uncle Buck for Professor Buchanan following a visit in 1902 by his nephew, Tom Matthews, the son of his sister Susan Ann Buchanan Matthews. His popularity extended both to students and to his colleagues, and his nickname became known across the state. University President William B. Bizzell recognized his contribution to raising the academic standards of the school.[12]

James Buchanan was a scholar as well. He had a passion for studying the career of Andrew Jackson from his home state of Tennessee. With his history colleague Edward Everett Dale, he wrote *A History of Oklahoma*, published in 1924 with reprints in several succeeding years through 1929. The book was dedicated to "the Pioneer Women of Oklahoma whose faith and toil have been such powerful factors in the building of a great commonwealth." In the preface the authors observe that

> *the experiences of one or the other of the authors have included ranching on the western prairies, the taking and improving of a claim, long years of teaching in country and village schools, membership in the Constitutional Convention, and many years of teaching history to college classes. Upon reflection it would seem that the authors' combined efforts should produce a book of Oklahoma history at least worthy of consideration.*[13]

Buchanan was a member of the Phi Beta Kappa honor society, the American Historical Society, the Mississippi Valley Historical Society, and Oklahoma Historical Society, serving on the board of directors of that organization from 1918 until his death in 1930. On the occasion of his death, the society adopted a resolution commending his service to the state and to the society.[14] During the Christmas season of 1929, Uncle Buck and his wife, Kathryn, visited John Price Buchanan on their way to a meeting of the American Historical Association. Both men were to die shortly, James at 65 and the governor at 83.

One of his colleagues remembered James Shannon Buchanan as the model academician:

First, he must be a good teacher. He must attract students, make his work interesting and build up a department. Then he must be a scholar, a research man. He must do things in his chosen field outside the four walls of the classroom. He must enlarge and enrich his profession and make a name and reputation for himself. And lastly, he must be willing to do the hundred-and-one things on the campus that someone must do, but that few people like to do. He must serve on committees, advise with students, look after details and help keep the wheels moving. In other words, he must be a faculty drudge. All of these things Professor Buchanan did and did well.[15]

THE BUCHANAN WOMEN AND BELMONT COLLEGE

John Price and James Shannon Buchanan's sister Jennie Thomas Buchanan, or Tommie, followed her brothers' lead in several respects. Twenty-one months older than James, Tommie followed John Price to Nashville to serve as his secretary during the Buchanan gubernatorial years. After the governor left office, Tommie joined the faculty of the new Belmont College for Women in Nashville. The school was founded in 1890 as an academy and two-year college on the estate of Adelicia Acklen, one of Tennessee's most prominent women of the 19th century.[16] The 1891 *Announcement and Prospectus* of Belmont College does not list any Buchanan as either staff or student. However, the 1895 copy of the same publication lists Tommie Buchanan as presiding teacher. Her obituary remembers her as "one of the most popular members of the faculty of that institution."

At some point around 1901, Tommie contracted tuberculosis and moved with her father, Thomas, to Norman, Oklahoma.[17] She continued to be listed among the Belmont faculty until 1904.[18] The family may have felt that Oklahoma's climate was better for her health than Tennessee's. Thomas died October 24, 1908, and Tommie died November 18, less than a month later.[19]

While Tommie was still at Belmont, her niece Rebecca Jane Buchanan, the second child and oldest daughter of John Price and Fannie Buchanan, joined her as a faculty member. Rebecca Jane, or Big Sister to the family, attended the Boston School of Expression, from which she graduated in 1899.[20] This interesting institution was founded in 1879 by Samuel Silas Curry, a native Tennessean, and its board members included Alexander Graham Bell, inventor of the telephone, and Charles W. Eliot, president of Harvard University. Remarkable for its time is the fact that its students included African-American women when most institutions of higher education were strictly segregated by race. In 1943 the Boston School of Expression was renamed Curry College, and it continues to operate today.[21]

After graduation from the Boston School, Rebecca Buchanan taught at Polytechnic College in Fort Worth, Texas, from 1899 to 1900 and Belmont College from 1900 to 1910.[22] The 1904 Belmont yearbook identifies Rebecca Jane Buchanan as "presiding teacher," and for the years 1906 through 1911, she is termed the "disciplinarian."[23] The 1905 yearbook lists neither Tommie nor Rebecca as faculty members, but there is no indication why Rebecca would not have been there.[24]

As disciplinarian it would have been Rebecca Jane's duty to see that the following student customs were observed.

- *Plans for daily exercise are rigidly executed.*
- *Borrowing and lending are firmly discouraged.*
- *Profuse or gaudy room decoration prohibited.*
- *Night study hall is kept for the benefit of the indolent or disorderly.*
- *No gentlemen callers received except by written parental permission, and then not oftener than once a month.*[25]

Fees were $350 for the year, which covered tuition for the basic courses, including English, Latin, and Greek, as well as board, laundry, electric lights, and steam heat.[26]

Whether or not she also had teaching responsibilities, Rebecca Jane clearly performed the duties appropriate to her title as revealed in excerpts from the diaries of Belmont students in 1908.

> *I am so mad with Miss Buchanan that I don't know what to do. Brother hasn't been out here but four times this week, and she positively refused to let him come out tonight.*
> —Beulah Long, November 15, 1908

> *When I played my new march in chapel today, it was so fast that the girls had to run, and Miss Buchanan called me down for breaking Belmont tradition.*
> —Bessie Smith, January 12, 1908

On the other hand, a kind word from her was appreciated.

> *Miss Buchanan has just complemented me on the correct shape which my uniform hat has retained during the wear of the Christmas holidays.*[27]
> —*Nolia Miller, March 1, 1908*

The younger daughters of John Price and Fanny followed their aunt and sister to Belmont. In 1904 Susan, or Susie to the family, Buchanan, seven years younger than Rebecca, appears as a "first-year senior." In that year Susie was the business manager of the *Blue and Bronze*, a student publication.[28] She does not appear again as a student. Susie later married Clift Epps, and when she, too, contracted TB, they moved to Texas seeking a better climate.[29]

In the 1905–1906 academic year, sister Frances at age 19 entered the sophomore class at Belmont. Frances was active in a number of school activities during her four years as a Belmont student. A classmate caught her in a high-spirited moment:

> *Frances Buchanan, as usual, took advantage of her sister's absence and made so much noise to-day [sic] in the dining room that Miss Golay had to tap the silence bell.*[30]

The 1909 yearbook lists Frances both as an "irregular" student and as a librarian. Beginning in 1911 Frances appears as postmistress for the college. She continued in that post for some time even after Rebecca left the school to move to Murfreesboro, Tennessee.[31]

MIDDLE TENNESSEE NORMAL SCHOOL

An essential milestone in the history of the state occurred when the Tennessee Legislature passed the General Education Bill of 1909, which authorized the creation of teacher-preparation institutions, or normal schools. The bill provided for one school in each of the three grand divisions of the state plus an agricultural and industrial normal school for African Americans.[32] Ultimately the result was a long-term connection between the Buchanan family and what would become Middle Tennessee State University. John Price Buchanan's daughter Rebecca would be a faculty member, and several of his grandchildren would attend the institution as students.

The Tennessee Board of Education appointed a committee of three men to assist the board in setting up the schools. Composing the committee were Andrew L. Todd of Murfreesboro, Robert L. Jones, and P. L. Harned. Todd was a prominent businessman and community leader in Murfreesboro, Jones was an educator, and Harned later became the first commissioner of education in Tennessee. The committee recommended Johnson City as the location for East Tennessee Normal and Memphis as the location of West Tennessee Normal. Murfreesboro was selected as the site for Middle Tennessee Normal rather than either Clarksville or Cookeville, and that selection was entirely due to Todd's efforts. Those other cities ultimately succeeded in acquiring their own schools. In 1914 with the support of Todd, a polytechnic institute was proposed for Cookeville, and Tennessee Polytechnic Institute became a reality in 1916. Austin Peay Normal School was established in Clarksville in 1927.³³

To promote the Murfreesboro site, the city council provided $80,000 for the purchase of land and buildings. The Rutherford County Court (now commission) voted, after some controversy, to add $100,000 to that sum. Andrew Todd played a role in the selection of the actual building site of the school on property east of the town limit. Eighty acres of farmland were donated at no cost to the state, and the state purchased 20 adjacent acres for $5,000. The school was to be constructed on the smaller site. A final agreement included provision for the building of streets and sewer lines.³⁴

The original campus buildings included the main administrative and instructional building, a girls' dormitory, a kitchen and dining hall, a powerhouse, and a home for the president. Smaller buildings housed farm equipment and animals to provide shelter for students' horses and buggies. For the first several years, male students lived in a rental house near campus.³⁵

Robert Lee Jones left the position of state superintendent of education to assume the role of first president of Middle Tennessee Normal School. His term of office began March 21, 1911, and he served until resigning to accept the position of superintendent of schools in Chattanooga in 1919. After the election of Alf Taylor as governor in 1920, Jones returned as president of Normal only to resign again in 1922 to become superintendent of city schools in Memphis.³⁶

On September 11, 1911, the school was dedicated, and classes met for the first time. As of the opening of classes, 125 students had enrolled in Normal, but that number increased by the second term of the year, bringing the total to 347 during the nine-month academic year. The largest enrollment occurred during the summer with teachers seeking to satisfy certification requirements. As a result, in the first complete year, 1,026 students attended the Normal.[37]

Given the scarcity of access to schools in the state with grades higher than eighth, the initial curriculum included a high school of four years and a teacher preparation or normal program of two years. A course in speaking was required in both years of the normal curriculum. This requirement would soon involve the Buchanans. [38]

One of those courses in speaking had the graphic title of "Pantomimic Training." Its description is taken from promotional literature for the school:

In training the body, exercises are given for poise, freedom and use. The two aims of this training are to secure normal adjustment of all the parts, and to fit the body as an agent of expression.[39]

To teach speaking and expression, the Middle Tennessee Normal English Department hired Rebecca Jane Buchanan. She taught reading and speech from 1913 to 1932. The 1914–1916 Normal *Bulletin* identifies six courses she offered. An entire section of the catalog is devoted to her area.

Between 1911 and 1925, 452 students received degrees from Middle Tennessee Normal, and more than 14,500 students "affiliated themselves with the institution."[40] During the 1920s the American Association of Teachers Colleges advocated an end to normal schools and the substitution of four-year colleges for teacher preparation. As a result, in the fall of 1925, the institution became Middle Tennessee State Teachers College.

Following the change in the status of the institution and its curriculum, an effort was made to improve the credentials of the faculty. Within two years the total size of the faculty increased by 50 percent, with most of the additions having master's degrees. For the first time the college added a faculty member with a doctoral degree. In 1929 the college took a major step when it was accredited by the Southern Association of Colleges and Secondary Schools.[41]

During these formative years of the school, Rebecca Buchanan was more than simply a classroom teacher. She founded and sponsored the school drama club, which was renamed the Buchanan Players in her honor in 1934, two years after she retired. From Normal's inception there had been student newspapers, first the *Signal* in the years 1912 to 1917, then the *Normalite* from 1921 to 1924, and finally the *Side-Lines* beginning in 1925. Rebecca served as faculty sponsor of the *Side-Lines*.[42]

Though the mission of the school focused on teacher training and demonstration classrooms existed from its opening, only in 1929 did the legislature appropriate money for the construction of a separate facility known as the Training School. The city of Murfreesboro donated 15 acres of land west of the campus. The building provided for 12 grades.[43]

In 1932, Rebecca Buchanan left the college due to illness. That year was a particularly difficult one for the institution as the country suffered through the Great Depression. To meet budgetary challenges the state board of education formed a retrenchment committee to determine a means of surviving the times. It is not clear whether the committee's recommended cutbacks played a role in Rebecca Jane's departure from the college or she left simply due to health problems.[44]

The institution underwent three more name changes over the years. In 1930 the name was changed to State Teachers College, Murfreesboro.[45] When the curriculum broadened and students lobbied for a new name in 1943, the name became Middle Tennessee State College. Twenty-two years later, in 1965, the institution assumed its present name, Middle Tennessee State University.[46]

THE SIXTH GENERATION OF BUCHANANS IN TENNESSEE

During the first three decades of the 20th century, the Buchanan family continued to be dominated by the presence of John Price Buchanan. The governor's farming enterprise could not support the entire group of nine children. His son Thomas Buchanan, named for his grandfather, farmed in Rutherford County, but the county tax records indicate that tax payments for farmland stopped in 1901. He became a Cumberland Presbyterian minister at the Old Beech Church in Sumner County, Tennessee, north of Nashville, and he died when struck by lightening while plowing at the early age of 38 in 1908. John Price Buchanan Jr., the second son, appears only briefly in the Rutherford County tax records. He tried the business world, but when that turned sour, he returned to farming. He was active in local politics in Manchester, Coffee County, Tennessee. As a political appointee, he became head of a Tennessee prison farm. Robert Norman Buchanan became a medical doctor in Hendersonville, Tennessee.[47]

There were four surviving daughters in the John Price Buchanan family. Susie, Frances, and Rebecca Jane Buchanan, the educator, have been described earlier. The fourth daughter, Maggie, died in the summer of 1900. After she left State Teachers College, Rebecca Jane Buchanan continued to teach speech and elocution privately for a number of years while living in Murfreesboro. She and her sister Frances lived together for many years in the home to which their parents had moved from the farm in 1925. When she died on June 23, 1965, many prominent citizens attended Rebecca Jane's funeral out of respect for her contributions to their education.[48]

The fourth son of John Price Buchanan, James McGill Buchanan, was born September 20, 1888. He was an athlete and followed his uncle James to the University of Oklahoma. During his two-year stay in Oklahoma, he ran track and played varsity football and baseball. By 1918 he had returned home, and the tax records of Rutherford County indicate that his father established him on 175 acres of what had been the family farm. He continued to pay taxes on that land until his father died in 1930. Despite what appeared to be a settlement of part of his property on this son, there was no transfer of title for that parcel of land. Consequently, records at the time of the governor's death show all of the Buchanan land as belonging to the "J. P. Buchanan heirs." Over this entire period, from his return from Oklahoma in 1918 until 1943, James Buchanan managed the entire family farm of 400 acres.

Jim Buchanan married Lila Herrin Scott in 1918. Lila

was born in Nashville to Thomas and Annie Marshall Scott on December 14, 1889. Thomas Scott was a deputy sheriff of Davidson County and died when Lila was a teenager. Lila graduated from Hume-Fogg High School in Nashville. This school, which continues to this day as one of the best high schools in Tennessee, was created in 1912 from the merger of two high schools: Hume, Nashville's oldest, and Fogg.[49] Rutherford County had no public high schools until the passage of the General Education Act of 1909. As a result high school graduates were rare.[50] With some rudimentary training, a high school graduate could become a certified teacher. Jim Buchanan and Lila Scott met during a period when she taught school in the Barfield community outside of Murfreesboro. The marriage produced three children: future Nobel Laureate James McGill Buchanan Jr. in 1919, Lila Scott Buchanan four years later, and Elizabeth in 1933. The family initially lived on the Big Creek Stock Buchanan farm, managed by Jim, in the Gum community south of Murfreesboro.

Like his father and his brother John Price Buchanan Jr., James—known as Jim Buck or Uncle Jim—was attracted to local politics. In 1926 he was elected to the Rutherford County Quarterly Court, which was the legislative body now known as the County Commission. For nearly 30 years James Buchanan continued to serve on the court, maintaining an almost perfect attendance record until the last year, 1953–1954, during which Lila became ill and died. Over the years he seldom took the lead in the court, but he represented the interests of his district. In particular, he championed the school serving the Gum community. The family had donated land at the corner of their property for the construction of a school along the Manchester highway. In the 1970s the John Price Buchanan School was moved to a new location about three miles closer to Murfreesboro, where it continues to operate as a Rutherford County elementary school. In 2011, the county opened an even newer campus for the Whitworth-Buchanan Middle School. At various times the school offered both primary and secondary grades. For the most part, Jim favored tight-fisted county budgets; however, he supported incentives for the location of a Carnation milk processing plant in the county. When told of this vote, his son, a libertarian and no friend of government subsidies for private interests, laughed and pointed out that the family sold milk to Carnation.[51]

Lila Buchanan, having been a teacher, exercised great influence on the education of her children. James Buchanan Jr. reports in his own autobiography that his mother, Lila, tutored him at home during several periods, allowing him to complete high school by the time he was 16 years old.[52] Both of the older children, James Jr. and Lila, known in the family as Bee, completed all of their formal primary and secondary schooling at the Buchanan School.

During the difficult years of the Great Depression, a family legend developed concerning the Buchanan "fortune." The story has a number of versions, but the essence was that an 18th-century Buchanan had owned extensive lands in New York City. After the Revolutionary War, the Buchanan owner had leased the property, and the lease was set to expire in about 1930. Supposedly the land would have been valued at $850 million, the proceeds from which would be distributed to anyone who could demonstrate kinship to the Buchanan family in Scotland. The story afforded the

Rutherford County, Tennessee, Buchanan family a dream of better times. Such tales have an appeal that causes them to persist, but by 1932 the legend had been discounted as untrue.[53]

In the early 1960s, a Buchanan family member in Tullahoma, Tennessee, contacted a friend and newly credentialed attorney, Thomas Wiseman, and asked him to investigate the legal claims to valuable property in New York City. Wiseman went to New York with that intent. Given that he received no money for his time or expenses, he economized by staying with a friend who lived in the city. The friend left Wiseman a key to allow him entry into the apartment. On opening the door, Wiseman received a heart-stopping shock when a kinkajou, a small animal related to raccoons and coatimundi, jumped on his shoulder.[54] His adventure in the wilds of New York City produced no evidence of any fortune or any legal basis for a claim to any property. Thomas Wiseman went on to become a U.S. Federal Judge and respected member of the Tennessee bar.[55]

When the Buchanan School was closed during World War II, Elizabeth, or Liz, Buchanan transferred to Central High School in Murfreesboro, from which she graduated in 1950. Liz says she was apprehensive about going to school with the town kids after her years in the Buchanan School, but she discovered that through her lessons in speech and elocution with her aunt, Rebecca Jane Buchanan, or "Big Sister," she not only knew some of the town kids but could compete with them academically. After graduation from high school, all three Buchanans went on to Middle Tennessee State, though between 1940 when James graduated and 1954 when Elizabeth graduated a different institutional name appeared on each of the diplomas.

In the 1930s Buchanan High School was known for its basketball teams. Lila, or Bee, played on a team that went to the state finals; the team star, Aileen Banks, went on to become an All-American at Nashville Business College.[56] When Bee graduated from Middle Tennessee State College in 1944, she went to work at the Murfreesboro Post Office and then to what is now the Oak Ridge National Laboratory. During World War II, Oak Ridge became a significant site employing many Tennesseans. It served as the project site for the production of uranium isotopes that were used to build atomic weapons for the war.[57] She also operated a private kindergarten long before public schools in Tennessee offered them. She met Thomas Graue while he was on maneuvers with the U.S. Army in middle Tennessee. Thomas was one of many Tennesseans who participated in the Tennessee maneuvers during the 1940s. Farmers whose land was often used for these maneuvers remember how the troops practiced driving tanks and performing other operations near their properties. The military staged training maneuvers in Tennessee because of the mild climate and varied terrain, similar to some of the landscapes and climates the soldiers would encounter in places overseas such as Europe.[58] Bee and Thomas married and spent their lives in Fayetteville, Arkansas, as loyal Razorback fans. Bee operated her own pre-school and worked at the University of Arkansas Library. They have one son, Douglas.[59]

After her graduation in 1954, Elizabeth Buchanan began a teaching career commuting to Davidson County to teach at the Mt. View School. She returned to Middle Tennessee State College to earn a Master of Arts degree

Figure 13. From left, Jeff Whorley, James M. Buchanan Jr., and Elizabeth Buchanan Bradley

in Education in 1959. She married John F. Whorley, and they had two sons, John F. Whorley Jr., or Jeff, in 1961 and James Marshall Whorley, or Jim, in 1963. When Jeff reached school age in 1966, Liz resumed her own teaching career by joining the faculty of the Middle Tennessee State University Campus School teaching first grade. Over the next 14 years, she introduced hundreds of Murfreesboro children to the wonders and challenges of school.

From its founding, a demonstration school was part of Middle Tennessee Normal. Originally known as the Training School, it was housed first at the Murfreesboro Public School, then in the Normal School administration building along with the rest of the Normal academic programs, next at a Murfreesboro school on East Main Street,

Figure 14. Homer Pittard Campus School, Murfreesboro

and finally in 1929 at its present location adjacent to the college campus. P. A. Lyon, the second president of Middle Tennessee State Teachers College and a good friend of Jim Buchanan Senior, had pressed for a new building for the Training School since 1922, and the legislature finally appropriated $10,500 to construct a building in 1928. The school was built on 10 acres donated to the college, and the construction costs totaled $140,000.[60]

In 1980 Elizabeth Buchanan Whorley became the director of the Campus School, and in 1985 the school was renamed the Homer Pittard Campus School to honor a Rutherford County educator. The school has always been a joint venture of sorts between the local school system and MTSU. In the early years it was a part of the Murfreesboro City Schools, but today it operates under a contract with the Rutherford County Board of Education. This relationship has always been a source of pride and of tension between the local school system, the local government, and MTSU. The Campus School faculty are members of the MTSU faculty, and the university supplements the salaries paid by the county system.[61]

Elizabeth Buchanan Whorley, now Bradley, retired from the Campus School in July 1985. She later moved to the Houston, Texas, area, where she enjoys her four grandchildren, golf, volunteer work, and Presbyterian Church activities.

THE CUMBERLAND PRESBYTERIAN CHURCH

The Cumberland Presbyterian Church has played a

significant role in the life of the Buchanan family. Perhaps from the creation of this church following the turn of the 19th century, family members have been communicants of the church, ministers of its preaching, and students at its institutions. Given that both the Presbyterian Church and the Buchanan family have their origins in Scotland, the association of the two is hardly surprising. The connection might be expected given the self-reliant nature of both this family and the Cumberland Presbyterians, who have contrasted themselves from the more Calvinistic Presbyterians by emphasizing an individual relationship with God.

Presbyterian congregations organized in Kentucky and Tennessee shortly after the first permanent settlers appeared in the Cumberland region. Initially the Cumberland region formed a synod of the Presbyterian Church in the new United States. With what is termed the Second Great Awakening, differences arose over some doctrinal issues among Presbyterian congregations. First was the matter of camp-meeting revivals, which established ministers often opposed.[62]

A second point of contention was ministerial education. Those inspired at camp meetings spread "the Word" among their neighbors. Revivalist ministers lacked formal education to the disdain of the seminary-educated establishment clergy. "Practices of ordination as well as theology were at stake, for since 1802 the Cumberland Presbytery had engaged in licensing uneducated but converted clergymen." This situation arose due to the practical reason that there were not enough educated men to meet the needs of congregations, but also there was "hostility between small farmer Presbyterians and the eastern-oriented church leadership."[63]

Among the earliest to join the Cumberland dissenters was Sugg's Creek Presbyterian Church, organized in 1800 in Wilson County, Tennessee. It became a Cumberland Presbyterian Church shortly after the Cumberland Presbytery was founded in February 1810. Family member James Marshall, father of Annie Marshall and grandfather of Lila Scott Buchanan, served as Sugg's Creek minister in 1887.[64] In nearby Arkansas, a Rev. John Buchanan, uncle of the Andrew H. Buchanan who taught at Cumberland University, was said by a late 19th-century writer to have done "more to Christianize Arkansas than any man who ever lived in that State."[65]

Deed records in Williamson County show that three acres were donated for a Cumberland Presbyterian Church in 1832.[66] A Robert G. Buchanan appears as an active member of the church in Franklin, Tennessee, throughout the middle of that century.[67] There were no Cumberland Presbyterian Churches in Rutherford County, Tennessee, until the 1830s, but a large camp meeting was held near Murfreesboro in 1820. By 1856 there were 19 Cumberland Presbyterian churches in Rutherford County that together could seat 3,550 people. Those numbers changed somewhat by 1890 when 18 churches served 1,467 members.[68] Lytle's Creek Cumberland Presbyterian Church was organized in 1836. It later moved further out Manchester Pike and changed its name to Mt. Tabor Cumberland Presbyterian Church, the church of the Buchanan family of Rutherford County.[69]

The church's first records from 1868 show Thomas Buchanan and John Price Buchanan both serving as elders. John Price Buchanan also served as an elder in the period from 1917 until his death. James M. Buchanan and Janie

Buchanan, secretary-treasurer, served on a building committee to help rebuild the church after it burned again in 1933. Tom Buchanan, John Price's oldest son, served as one of its pastors.[70] The current brick sanctuary south of Murfreesboro was built in 1966 and continues to serve a small congregation. Many family members rest in the Mt. Tabor graveyard adjacent to the church and south of Murfreesboro.

At the midpoint of the 20th Century, the Buchanans of middle Tennessee had already accumulated a rich history. Although this family never claimed to be of the highest social class in the state, it undeniably ranks among the families that made the prosperity and stability of Tennessee possible. It only remained for another family scholar to add further distinction to the Buchanan reputation.

NOTES

1. It now operates according to its public records as a private, independent liberal arts institution.

2. Andrew H. Buchanan was the son of Isaac and Naomi Crawford Buchanan in Washington County, AR. Isaac had been killed by Indians allied with federal troops during the Civil War, and three of Andrew's brothers (William M, Buchanan, Pleasant W, Buchanan, and James G. Buchanan) all lost their lives in the service of the Confederacy at Cane Hill, AR. Andrew and his wife, Malinda A. Alexander, had nine children, five of whom survived to adulthood. They were James C., Andrew B., Isaac W. P., Kate Stewart, and Blanche Alexander Buchanan. The first is known to have been an engineer and the second a Cumberland Presbyterian minister. Andrew Buchanan is known for his work with the United States Coast and Geodetic Survey, which included work in helping to settle the boundary line between Tennessee and Virginia, and for his devotion to the Cumberland Presbyterian Church. See William S. Speer, *Sketches of Prominent Tennesseans*, Nashville, TN, Albert B. Tavel, 1888, pp. 148–149.

   In 1929, the city of Lebanon, TN, elected a Frank Buchanan, who may have been a descendant, as mayor on a reform ticket pledged to assure the city adequate water supplies and firefighting equipment. See Frank Burns, *Wilson County* (Memphis, TN: Memphis State University Press, 1983), pp. 74–75.

   It may well be that Andrew Buchanan was related to the John Buchanan family. Andrew's grandmother Jane Neely Buchanan's name appears in the *1770–1790 Census of the Cumberland Settlements* (Tennessee State Library and Archives).

3. The Cornersville Institute was founded in 1854. After several modifications the property was turned over to the city of

Cornersville and then to Marshall County. The present Cornersville High School is on the property on which the Institute was built in 1856 (*http://cvhs.marshall.k12tn.net/mission/chshistory.html*).

4. Watkins Institute was founded in 1885 as a school for "those in need." Today it is Watkins College of Art, Design & Film, *http://www.watkins.edu/about-watkins/watkins-brief-history*, retrieved August 16, 2012. National Bureau of Economic Research, "NBER Macrohistory, VIII Income and Employment," *http://www.nber.org/databases/macrohistory/contents/chapter08.html*, retrieved August 23, 2010.

5. *http://digital.library.okstate.edu/chronicles/v008/v008p350.html*, *http://oklahomarelocation.net/history.html*, retrieved July 24, 2007. William Bennett Bizzell and others, *An Appreciation of James Shannon Buchanan* (Norman, OK: University of Oklahoma, 1930), pp. 8–9.

6. *http://www.ou.edu/content/web/about_ou/tradition.html*, retrieved June 20, 2012.

7. *http://catalog.ou.edu/current/Philosophy.htm*, retrieved June 20, 2012.

8. The president of the university and a number of faculty were fired when a new governor of Oklahoma was elected in 1922 (Roy Gittinger, "The Class of 1924," *Sooner Magazine*, January 1950, p. 17).

9. Bizzell, *An Appreciation*, pp. 19–20.

10. *http://digital.library.okstate.edu/encyclopedia/entries/e/en001.html*, retrieved August 16, 2012.

11. James Shannon Buchanan and Edward Everett Dale, *A History of Oklahoma* (New York: Row Peterson & Company, 1924), pp. 278–279.

12. Bizzell, *An Appreciation*, pp. 11, 16.

13. Buchanan and Dale, *A History of Oklahoma*, pp. iii, v.

14. Chronicles of Oklahoma, *http://digital.library.okstate.edu/ chronicles/v008/v008p350.html*.

15. Bizzell, *An Appreciation*, p. 17. The Buchanan Years, *http:// digital.libraries.ou.edu/sooner/articles/p46-47_1965v38n1_ OCR.pdf*, retrieved August 16, 2012.

16. "In the mid-1800s, the campus was known as Adelicia Acklen's Belle Monte estate. The antebellum mansion remains today, flanked by university buildings separated in age by a century. The first educational institution on the estate was the original Belmont College (1890–1913), offering elementary school through junior college education to young ladies. The school merged with Ward Seminary to become the prestigious Ward-Belmont School for Women (1913–1951) and in 1951 became the coed Belmont College. In 1991, the college became Belmont University and, this year, began the 114th year of higher education on this site." Source: *http://www.belmont.edu/umac/belmont_ history/index.html*.

17. "Estimable Women Dies in Oklahoma," *Nashville Banner*, November 19, 1908. Tommie's obituary states that she had been in Oklahoma for "seven or eight years," which would have meant they moved there about 1901.

18. The 1904 yearbook, the *Aitrop* (Belmont University Special Collections) lists among the "staff of instruction" J. T. Buchanan, on leave, and R. J. Buchanan, presiding teacher.

19. Obituary for Thomas Buchanan, *Franklin Review Appeal*; "Estimable Woman Dies in Oklahoma," *Nashville Banner*, November 19, 1908.

20. Middle Tennessee Normal School *Bulletin*, 1914–1916, p. 7. In the Belmont publications Rebecca Jane's only academic credential listed was the Boston School, but beginning in 1910 "Graduate Belmont College" is added to the list. The earliest surviving documents for the college are for 1890–1891, 1895, and 1904, and none report Rebecca as a student or graduate. Clearly she may have attended during the missing years.

21. *http://www.acsu.buffalo.edu/~duchan/new_history/women_profession.html*; *http://www.curry.edu/about-curry/our-legacy/history.html*, retrieved June 20, 2012.

22. MTSNS *Bulletin*, Vol. IV, No. 1, 1913–1914.

23. MTSNS *Bulletin*, 1914–1916, p. 7. *Milady in Brown*, various years (Belmont University Library Special Collections).

24. *Milady in Brown*, 1905 (Belmont University Library Special Collections).

25. "Some Student Customs and Suggestions to Possible Patrons," *Prospectus*, Belmont College for Young Women (undated but at least by 1911), p. 27 (Belmont University Library Special Collections).

26. Ibid., p. 24.

27. "Sub Senior Diary by Ouida Labit," *Milady in Brown*, 1908 (Belmont University Library Special Collections).

28. The 1904 *Airtrop* (Belmont University Library Special Collections). The exact structure of classes is not clear from the surviving materials, but since the institution was both a high school and a two-year college it seems likely that a first-year senior was a fourth-year, or senior, high school student.

29. Interview with James M. Buchanan Jr., May 16, 2007, Indianapolis, IN.

30. "Sub Senior Diary," *Milady in Brown*, 1908 (Belmont University Library Special Collections).

31. *Prospectus*, Belmont College for Young Women, undated but at least by 1911 (Belmont University Library Special Collections), lists Rebecca J. Buchanan as disciplinarian and Frances Buchanan as postmistress. *Announcement and Prospectus, 1912* (Belmont University Library Special Collections) lists Frances Buchanan as postmistress but does not list Rebecca J. Buchanan in any capacity.

32. Homer Pittard, *The First Fifty Years* (Murfreesboro, TN: Middle Tennessee State College, 1961), p. 9.

33. Ibid., pp. 9–11; *www.tntech.edu*, retrieved July 26, 2007; *www.apsu.edu*, retrieved July 26, 2007.

34. Pittard, *The First Fifty Years*, pp. 13–14, 18–19.

35. Ibid., pp. 22–23. Of the original buildings the administration building, today known as Kirksey Old Main, the girls' dorm, and the president's home all remain in use.

36. Ibid., pp. 32, 110–119.

37. Ibid., pp. 52, 55, 89–91.

38. Ibid., p. 60.

39. Ibid., p. 61.

40. Ibid., pp. 126–127.

41. Ibid., pp. 128–129, 130.

42. Ibid., pp. 66–69, 131.

43. Ibid., pp. 135–136.

44. Interview with James M. Buchanan Jr., May 16, 2007, Indianapolis, IN.

45. *Bulletin*, State Teachers College, Murfreesboro (1930, p. 14).

46. Pittard, *The First Fifty Years*, pp. 136, 173.

47. Interview with James M. Buchanan Jr., May 16, 2007, Indianapolis, IN.

48. Frances Buchanan had an unsuccessful marriage and spent much of her life working as an accountant, first at J. C.

Penney in Murfreesboro and then at the Rutherford Hospital. Correspondence with Elizabeth Buchanan Bradley, September 14, 2007; obituary, *Daily News Journal*, June 24, 1965.

49. Correspondence with James M. Buchanan Jr., August 2, 2007. Source: *http://www.humefogghs.mnps.org/Page504.aspx*, retrieved August 3, 2007.

50. "Education in Rutherford County," Sims, *A History of Rutherford County*, p. 167.

51. Interview with James M. Buchanan Jr., May 16, 2007, Indianapolis, IN.

52. James M. Buchanan, *Better Than Plowing and Other Personal Essays* (Chicago: University of Chicago Press, 1992), pp. 27–28.

53. Patty Hopkinson, "The Buchanan Estate Scam," *Buchanan Banner*, Vol. 25 (4), Winter 1997, *http://www.geocities.com/ genealogist@sbcglobal.net/scam.html*, retrieved February 16, 2007; "Inquiry Fails to Unearth Trace of Buchanan Estate," *Houston Chronicle*, January 20, 1932.

54. Kinkajous are generally quiet and docile, and they have no noticeable odor. Because they are slow and languid, especially just after being wakened from a nap, they do not particularly like quick sudden movements. As a rule, Kinkajous are gentle and nonaggressive most of the time, although they can get wound up and become quite playful, and like to "dive bomb" and pounce on you from high places! Source: *http://www.juliesjungle.com/ kinkajou.php*, retrieved August 6, 2007.

55. Correspondence with the Honorable Thomas A. Wiseman Jr., February 23, 2007.

56. She played for the college from 1943 to 1945, for Vultee Aircraft from 1943 to 1945, for the Goldbloomers in 1946, for the Atlanta Sports Arena Blues from 1947 to 1948, and again for Nashville Business College from 1949 to 1950. See Rebekah Hurst, "Noah's All-American Star: Coffee County Is Home to Women's Basketball Legend Alline Banks-Sprouse," *Manchester Times*, September 5, 2007, pp. 1A, 5A.

57. For more on the history of Oak Ridge, TN, see Charles Johnson, *City Behind a Fence: Oak Ridge, Tennessee, 1942–1946* (Knoxville, TN: University of Tennessee Press, 1981) and Leland Johnson and Daniel Schaffer, *Oak Ridge National Laboratory: The First Fifty Years* (Knoxville, TN: University of Tennessee Press, 1994).

58. Patricia B. Howard, "World War II," *Tennessee Encyclopedia of History & Culture*, ed. Carroll Van West (Nashville, TN: Rutledge Hill Press, 1998), 1080–1084. For more on the Tennessee maneuvers, see Eugene Sloan, *With the Second Army Somewhere in Tennessee* (Murfreesboro, TN: Middle Tennessee State College, 1956).

59. Correspondence with Elizabeth Buchanan Bradley, September 14, 2007.

60. Jennifer Martin, "On the National Register: Campus School Complex Dates from 1929," *Murfreesboro Post*, www.murfreesboropost.com/news.php?viewStory=2871, retrieved July 30, 2007.

61. Ibid.

62. B. W. McDonnold, *History of the Cumberland Presbyterian Church*, 4th edition (Nashville, TN: Board of Publication of Cumberland Presbyterian Church, 1899), pp. 39, 41.

63. Dickson D. Bruce Jr., *And They Sang Hallelujah: Plain-Folk Camp-Meeting Religion, 1800–1845* (Knoxville, TN: University of Tennessee Press, 1974), pp. 41–42.

64. Thomas E. Partlow, *Sugg's Creek Cumberland Presbyterian Church: An Early History* (Lebanon, TN.: Thomas E. Partlow, 1974), pp. 5, 27.

65. Speer, *Sketches of Prominent Tennesseans*, p. 148.

66. Williamson County, TN, Deed Book L, p. 397 (Williamson County, TN, Archives)

67. Cumberland Presbyterian Church vertical file (Williamson County, TN, Archives).

68. Robert E. Corlew and Mary S. Corlew, *A History of the Cumberland Presbyterian Church at Murfreesboro, Tennessee* (Murfreesboro, TN, September 1, 1956), pp. 6, 9.

69. Carlton C. Sims (ed.), *A History of Rutherford County* (Murfreesboro, TN: Carlton C. Sims, 1947), p. 181.

70. Mrs. Robert Ralph, "History of Mt. Tabor Cumberland Presbyterian Church Begins in 1836," Rutherford County Historical Society.

CHAPTER VII.

JAMES M. BUCHANAN JR.

Learning is not attained by chance; it must be sought for with ardor and attended to with diligence.
—*Abigail Adams*

HIS WORK

James Buchanan told us that at State Teachers College in Murfreesboro and at the University of Tennessee his instincts were for scholarship, not necessarily economics. He had not yet pursued economics with a passion. Once he found himself at the University of Chicago, that changed. He related the story in a lecture given following his receipt of the Nobel Prize:

> *I was specifically asked to discuss my evolution as an economist, an assignment that I cannot fulfill. I am not a "natural economist" as some of my colleagues are, and I did not "evolve" into an economist. Instead I sprang full blown upon intellectual conversion, after I "saw the light." I was indeed converted by Frank Knight.*[1]

He was inspired by Knight's own lecture on the role and nature of markets. One more important contribution that Knight made to Buchanan's intellectual development concerns his willingness to challenge established ideas. Perhaps this independent mind can be traced to Buchanan's upbringing, but Knight confirmed the importance of it for the dedicated scholar:[2]

> *He almost single-mindedly conveyed the message that there exists no god whose pronouncements deserve elevation to the sacrosanct, whether god within or without the scientific academy. Everything, everyone, anywhere, anytime—all is open to challenge and criticism. There is a moral obligation to reach one's own conclusions, even if this sometimes means exposing the prophet whom you have elevated to intellectual guruship.*

As discussed previously, Buchanan's early career was spent in Tennessee and Florida. The important step in his career path came in 1956, when he joined the faculty of the University of Virginia in Charlottesville. Virginia is a storied institution that Thomas Jefferson founded in 1819 and on whose board of visitors James Madison had served. Madison in particular ranks among Buchanan's most respected historical figures.

The move to Virginia constituted another of the major crossroads in his life. At that juncture he was offered the opportunity to return to the University of Chicago as a faculty member, a flattering invitation. Instead, he chose his own path, to establish a reputation for himself. He explains that decision in his own words:[3]

> *It has allowed me to work somewhat more independently, to develop my own ideas rather than in a cocoon of people who were so dominant that they would have made it difficult for me to be as independent. . . . I did have an opportunity to go back to the University of Chicago, but I'm glad that I didn't.*

In Charlottesville he met and began to collaborate with a group that formed the basis of a perspective of economics now called *public choice*. Among that group was Gordon Tullock, who came to Virginia to do postdoctoral research in 1958 after earning a law degree at the University of Chicago. These two men formed a partnership that proved important for both careers. In 1962 they published *The Calculus of Consent*, which has become the best-known publication for each.[4]

On the question of the origins of the name *public choice*, Buchanan related the following:[5]

> *That is an interesting story in the sense that Gordon Tullock and I organized in 1963 this little research program in Charlottesville. We brought together people [at the Old Ivy Inn in Charlottesville, Virginia] working in these areas trying to analyze institutional behavior outside of normal market behavior. We had people from different areas come, from political science, sociology, and economists, about 15 or 16, and we just exchanged research ideas. Obviously there was some common thread going through all of this. And so we decided that we wanted to continue and have some organization. . . . We came up with the name "The Committee on Non-*

Market Decision-Making." . . . [Still later] we had the fourth meeting of the group—I think this was in '67—at Roosevelt University in Chicago. We devoted one afternoon session to trying to come up with a better title. . . . At the best of my recollection . . . the name itself came from a political scientist at the University of Oregon named William Mitchell. He came up with the notion of Public Choice. . . . From that time on we changed the Committee on Non-Market Decision-Making into the Public Choice Society, and we called the journal Public Choice.

For a number of years, Buchanan was able to attract many visiting scholars and exceptional graduate students to Charlottesville. But as the passions of the 1960s heated, he encountered opposition from other faculty members on the campus. "We were hated with a passion by other faculty on the campus." The economics department was "interpreted by other faculty as right-wing fascists."[6]

That charge is patently ridiculous for a libertarian, who champions individual liberty, free economic exchange, and the idea that no member of society should be coerced. Perhaps it is the perception that free economic exchange means subservience to business interests that leads to confusion about libertarians. In fact, students of public choice would see the opportunity of some business interests to capture benefits from other members of society through government processes as anathema.

Ultimately Buchanan left the University of Virginia in 1968 because of what he described as "problems with the university administration."[7] After a year at the University of

California, Los Angeles, Buchanan became "horrified" with that faculty and administration. Recalling the late 1960s and early 1970s, when California campuses were often in a state of turmoil over protests against the war in Vietnam and cultural changes, Buchanan referred to protests that "reached the limits of theatrical absurdity."[8] He then returned east to the mountains at Virginia Polytechnic Institute and State University, or Virginia Tech, in Blacksburg. The remoteness from the chaos of California and the venom of Charlottesville appealed to him as well as the orderliness of the community.[9] There he, Tullock, and others reconnected and established the Center for the Study of Public Choice, which became a focal point for like-minded scholars who looked to James Buchanan as their mentor.

Over the years, differences in the vision for the economics program between Buchanan's colleagues and Virginia Tech administrators precipitated another move. In 1983, with an opportunity to join the entrepreneurial group of faculty and administrators at George Mason University, Buchanan and the center relocated to Fairfax, Virginia, where the center remains today.[10]

As discussed at the beginning of the book, on October 16, 1986, James M. Buchanan was notified he had been awarded the Nobel Prize. His comment, "If I can win the Nobel Prize, you can get a Nobel Prize," was not to diminish his own achievement but rather to emphasize that someone not born into high social status or affiliated with a prestigious university can still attain such recognition as a Nobel Prize with dedication and hard work.

Figure 15. Nobel Prize in Economic Science

His Views on the World

Public choice explores the motivation of individuals making decisions about public investments and taxation, among other topics. The basic idea is that people behave similarly in making decisions regarding collective or public goods and services as when making decisions in their personal life.

What are the essential elements of public choice and Buchanan's approach to economics? He identified three fundamental aspects of his research program, which he called the "hard core." In his own words:

> *The hard core in public choice can be summarized in three presuppositions: (1) methodological individualism, (2) rational choice, and (3) politics as exchange.*[11]

In methodological individualism, the basis for analysis is the motivation of the individual. In fact this approach underlies much of modern economics, the idea that individuals make decisions by evaluating the costs and benefits to themselves of the alternatives they face. Buchanan was quick to add that this notion does not imply that individuals act in "isolation from and apart from the community" or other individuals, but it is in contrast to an approach that would assume some kind of a group or collective consciousness, such as "society" or "the state," in a public, collective, or government decision-making situation.[12]

Rational choice refers to the idea that individuals are "capable of choosing among alternatives in [a] sufficiently orderly manner." Once again, this concept is fundamental to modern economic analysis. The presumption is that in choosing among alternatives the individual is able to order his preferences based on all of the factors that may influence him and not some conception of "rationality" imposed by the economist.[13]

The third element of the *hard core* of public choice is politics as exchange:

> *Men co-operate through exchange of goods and services in organized markets, and such co-operation implies*

> mutual gain. *The individual enters into an exchange relationship in which he furthers his own interest by providing some product or service that is of direct benefit to the individual on the other side of the transaction. At base, political or collective action under the individualistic view of the State is much the same. Two or more individuals find it mutually advantageous to join forces to accomplish certain common purposes. In a very real sense, they "exchange" inputs in the securing of the commonly shared output.*[14]

For Buchanan exchange was the very heart of economics and essential to his political economy. He used the analogy of the fictional character Robinson Crusoe from Daniel Defoe's novel of the same name to make this point. Alone on his island, Crusoe faces decisions about how best to utilize his time. In economics this situation would be a problem of maximizing his well-being, something that traditional economics books would offer as the definition of economics. Buchanan argued, in contrast, that it is only when Friday arrives on Crusoe's island that "the uniquely symbiotic aspects of behavior . . . arise . . . and Crusoe is forced into *association* with another human being. The fact of association requires that a wholly different, and wholly new, sort of behavior take place, that of 'exchange,' 'trade,' or 'agreement.'"[15]

This mutual exchange between individuals would follow from the basic proposition of libertarians that there is no justification for one person to coerce another person. For that reason a foundation of his views on collective decision-making is that there should be, to the greatest extent possible, a consensus on a set of rules within which individually or collectively people are allowed "to pursue [their] desired ends." In other words, there should be a constitution that specifies the *process* by which we make decisions.

In Buchanan's terms this issue introduces *constitutional economics*. He used the analogy of a poker game. All the players must know the rules and determine their strategy in any particular hand within those rules. The rules can be changed only if all agree and then only in a later hand, not in the middle of the current hand. In "ordinary" economics the focus is on the strategy within the rules that have been determined beforehand. Constitutional economics focuses on the process for determining those rules. The Constitution of the United States lays out the rules within which the executive, legislative, and judicial arms of our government propose, enact, and enforce the laws we follow. In order to change the process, it is necessary to revise or amend the Constitution. It is in this later step that constitutional economics analyzes the costs and benefits of alternative sets of rules.

As in a poker game, people can play only if they agree to abide by the rules. By the same token, citizens should agree to the rules set forth in a constitution. There must be consensus, or nearly so, in order for the constitution to succeed. Through such a consensus, people recognize that it is sometimes in their interest to accept constraints or limits on their behavior, in effect submitting to coercion.[16]

The point has been made that James Buchanan was never a political creature; rather, he was a scholar. That does not mean he was reticent to express his own views. On the basis of his analysis of the alternatives, Buchanan is on record as supporting three amendments to the U.S. Constitution. The first he termed a fiscal responsibility amendment that would require a balanced federal budget. The second he described as prohibiting discrimination through political coercion. In this instance his argument was that the ideals of democracy—for example, that all are created equal before the law—should be upheld in practice as well as in principle. He asked, "Why is discrimination in political action constitutionally permissible whereas discrimination in law is out of bounds?" Here he admitted that the wording of such an amendment would be challenging. The third amendment would prohibit intervention in voluntary exchanges either in the domestic economy or in international exchange. In other words, this amendment would dictate open economic markets.[17] With regard to the latter amendment, he recognized that there may be exchanges that we do not want to take place but that there should be constitutional consensus on a set of rules by which we can permit or prohibit certain exchanges.[18]

More of James Buchanan's ideas and contributions are included in Appendix A. It takes the form of questions posed by the authors with responses drawn from Buchanan's various works.

After he received the Nobel Prize, Jim Buchanan was invited to lecture all over the world. In addition he continued to publish and collaborate with his many students, colleagues, and those interested in his research program. Although his schedule slowed over the years, he continued to pursue the life of a scholar into his 10th decade. Buchanan served as Advisory General Director of the Center for Study of Public Choice and Distinguished Professor Emeritus of Economics at George Mason University. James McGill

Buchanan died January 9, 2013, in Blacksburg, Virginia, after a brief illness. He was fully engaged in his latest projects through the last month of his life.

In 2007, Middle Tennessee State University, where Buchanan first matriculated, designated the top 20 incoming scholars in its Honors College as Buchanan Scholars, in special recognition of one of the university's most illustrious graduates. Each recipient is awarded a full scholarship to the university. The Buchanan family motto, *Clarior Hinc Honos* ("Brighter Hence the Honor"), is incorporated into the certificate awarded to each new honoree.[19]

Figure 16. Nobel Prize winner James M. Buchanan Jr.

Notes

1. James Buchanan's October 1987 lecture at Trinity University (*http://www.trinity.edu/nobel/*).

2. Frank Knight was a faculty member in economics at the University of Chicago from 1929 to 1955. Knight is credited with being a founder of the Chicago School of Economics. He taught many of the most highly regarded 20th-century economists including Nobel laureates Milton Friedman and James Buchanan. *http://www.econlib.org/library/Enc/bios/Knight.html*, retrieved January 8, 2007.

3. Geoffrey Brennan, *A Conversation with James M. Buchanan*, Parts 1 and 2 (Liberty Fund, Inc., 2001) (DVD).

4. James M. Buchanan and Gordon Tullock, *The Calculus of Consent: Logical Foundations of Constitutional Democracy* (Ann Arbor, MI: University of Michigan Press, 1962).

5. Interview with Dr. Buchanan, December 1, 2006, Blacksburg, VA.

6. Brennan, *A Conversation with James Buchanan*.

7. Buchanan, *Better Than Plowing*, p. 100.

8. Ibid., p. 114.

9. Brennan, *A Conversation with James M. Buchanan*.

10. George Mason University is named after an American founding father best known for drawing up Virginia's Declaration

of Rights.

11. "Public Choice: The Origins and Development of a Research Program," *http://www.pubchoicesoc.org/about_pc.html*, retrieved November 28, 2006.

12. "The Domain of Constitutional Political Economy," Chapter 1, *The Economics and the Ethics of Constitutional Order* (Ann Arbor, MI: University of Michigan Press, 1991), p. 14.

13. "The Domain of Constitutional Political Economy," *loc. cit.*, p. 16.

14. Buchanan and Tullock, *The Calculus of Consent*, p. 18.

15. "What Should Economists Do?" *Southern Economic Journal* 30 (January 1964), pp. 213–222.

16. Buchanan, James M., *The Economics and the Ethics of Constitutional Order* (Ann Arbor, MI: The University of Michigan Press, 1991).

17. "Three Amendments: Responsibility, Generality, and Natural Liberty," *http://www.cato-unbound.org/2005/12/05/james-m-buchanan/three-amendments/*, retrieved February 9, 2011.

18. Brennan, *A Conversation with James M. Buchanan*.

19. Dr. Buchanan was on hand for the installation of the first class, which included a celebration of his 88th birthday. At the time his nephew, Jeff Whorley, served as chair of the newly created Honors College Board of Visitors.

CHAPTER VIII.

Epilogue

The story of the Buchanan family is essentially American because the family succeeded without the benefits of an Old World aristocratic heritage or a New World fortune. The Buchanan family is representative of Tennessee and American successes—derived from a system of law that guarantees economic, political, and religious freedom and fosters education. The Buchanan story is one of a family with the courage, strength of character, independence, and steadfastness to build new communities of people and ideas.

From the middle of the 18th century through the first decade of the 21st century, the Buchanan family has demonstrated an ability to lead its community and its contemporaries. Whether by necessity or a desire to improve their lot in life, Buchanans left their native Scotland for Ireland, a place difficult for any to prosper. Again by necessity or the opportunity for a new beginning, the family moved to the new land of North America. Evidence suggests that wherever they located they found some success, but again they moved to the next frontier of the western colonies. From there they actually pushed the frontier themselves by locating along the Cumberland River. Not only did they have to create an entirely new home from the forest, but they had to defend their right to be there from the native people who rejected that right.

Once established in Tennessee, the Buchanans thrived and impressed their neighbors with their character. Over the course of the 19th century, through good times and bad, war and peace, they exhibited resilience and independence. One small farm family in Williamson County, Tennessee, produced three children who influenced their time and place during a period of great transition in the country. In his own fashion John Price Buchanan stood up for his principles even when faced with challenges that overwhelmed him. James Shannon Buchanan moved still further west to help create a new state and build a university. At a time when women typically managed the home, raised children, and often died in childbirth, Tommie Buchanan gained an education, taught in pioneering women's colleges, and supported her aged father. Many other less-heralded Buchanans provided the resources and support that allowed others to excel.

Without the advantage of family wealth or great prestige, James McGill Buchanan Jr. carried on in the spirit of his family by pioneering a new field of economics. Preferring to make his own reputation with hard work and his independent mind, James Buchanan eschewed the offers of elite universities to build a program of research that earned him a Nobel Prize. Along his path he attracted a group of scholars who will continue to develop and cultivate the ideas he inspired.

It cannot be known how James Buchanan would have fared without his particular family background, but there is continuity in this story. James Buchanan shared these traits with his Buchanan forebearers: he was a disciplined, hard-working, motivated individual who followed the path he chose for himself.

BIBLIOGRAPHY

1850 U.S. Census, Williamson County, 8th Civil District, TN.

1860 U.S. Census, Williamson County, Eastern Subdistrict, TN.

1870 U.S. Census, Williamson County, 8th Civil District, TN.

Acklen, Jeannette Tillotson. *Bible Records and Marriage Bonds*. Nashville: Clearfield Co. and reprinted by Genealogical Publishing Co. 1995.

Annable, Edward C. Jr. "A History of the Roads of Rutherford County Tennessee, 1804–1878." M.A. Thesis, Middle Tennessee State University, December 1982.

"Appropriations Bill." *Acts of Tennessee 1889*. Nashville, TN: Marshall & Bruce, 1889.

Arnow, Harriet Simpson. *Flowering of the Cumberland*. New York: Macmillan, 1963.

———. "The Pioneer Farmer and His Crops in the Cumberland Region." *Tennessee Historical Quarterly*, Vol. XIX, No. 4 (December 1960).

———. *Seedtime on the Cumberland*. New York: Macmillan, 1960.

Ash, Steven V. *Middle Tennessee Society Transformed, 1860–1870: War and Peace in the Upper South*. Baton Rouge, LA: Louisiana State University Press, 1988.

Atkins, Jonathan. "Politicians, Parties, and Slavery: The Second Party System and the Decision for Disunion in Tennessee." In *Tennessee History: The Land, the People, and the Culture*, ed. Carroll Van West. Knoxville, TN: University of Tennessee Press, 1998.

Barnes, Donna A. "Farmers' Alliance." *Handbook of Texas Online*, http://www.tsha.utexas.edu/handbook/online/articles/FF/aaf2.html, retrieved July 9, 2007.

Barnes, Katherine R. "James Robertson's Journey to Nashville: Tracing the Route of Fall 1779." *Tennessee Historical Quarterly* 35 (Summer 1976): 145–161.

Bergeron, Paul H., et al. *Tennesseans and Their History*. Knoxville, TN: University of Tennessee Press, 1999.

"A Big Boycott Proposed." *New York Times*. August 13, 1890: 1.

Bigger, Jeanne R. "Jack Daniel Distillery and Lynchburg: A Visit to Moore County, Tennessee." *Tennessee Historical Quarterly* 31 (Spring 1972): 3–21.

Biographical Directory, Tennessee General Assembly, 1796–1967. (Preliminary, No. 6) Rutherford County.

Bizzell, William Bennett, et al. *An Appreciation of James Shannon Buchanan.* Norman, OK: University of Oklahoma, 1930.

Bockstruck, Lloyd Dewitt. *Virginia's Colonial Soldiers.* Baltimore, MD: Genealogical Publishing, 1998.

Brandon, Helen Hartman. *Hartman-Buchanan Family.* Murfreesboro, TN: H. H. Brandon, October 1988. Tennessee State Library and Archives Collection, Nashville, TN.

Brennan, Geoffrey. *A Conversation with James M. Buchanan*, Parts 1 and 2. Liberty Fund, Inc., 2001.

Bruce, Dickson D., Jr. *And They Sang Hallelujah: Plain-Folk Camp Meeting Religion, 1800–1845.* Knoxville, TN: University of Tennessee Press, 1974.

The Buchanan Name in History. Provo, UT: The Generations Network, 2005.

"Buchanan Still Leads." *New York Times*, July 18, 1890: 5.

Buchanan, James M. *Better Than Plowing and Other Personal Essays*. Chicago: University of Chicago Press, 1992.

_____. *Economics from the Outside In: Better Than Plowing and Beyond*. College Station, TX: Texas A&M Press, 2001.

_____. *The Economics and the Ethics of Constitutional Order*. Ann Arbor, MI: The University of Michigan Press, 1991.

_____. *Why I, Too, Am Not a Conservative*: The Normative Vision of Classical Liberalism. Northampton, MA: Edward Elgar Publishing, 2005.

Buchanan, James M., and Gordon Tullock. *The Calculus of Consent: Logical Foundations of Constitutional Democracy*. Ann Arbor, MI: University of Michigan Press, 1962.

Buchanan, James Shannon, and Edward Everett Dale. *A History of Oklahoma*. New York: Row Peterson & Company, 1924.

Burns, Frank. *Wilson County*. Memphis, TN: Memphis State University Press, 1983.

Caldwell, Mary French. *Tennessee: The Volunteer State*. Chicago. IL: Richtext Press, 1968.

"The Complete George Washington Papers," Library of Congress, *http://memory.loc.gov/ammem/gwhtml/gwhome.html*, retrieved September 26, 2007.

Cooper, William J. Jr., and Thomas E. Terrill. *The American South: A History*, 2nd ed. New York: McGraw-Hill, 1996.

Corlew, Robert E. *Tennessee: A Short History*, 2nd ed. Knoxville, TN: University of Tennessee Press, 1981.

Corlew, Robert E., and Mary S. *A History of the Cumberland Presbyterian Church at Murfreesboro, Tennessee*. Murfreesboro, TN, September 1, 1956.

Correspondence with the Honorable Thomas A. Wiseman Jr., February 23, 2007.

Crutchfield, James A. *Yesteryear in Nashville: An Almanac of Nashville History*, Franklin, TN: J. A. Crutchfield, Privately Published, 1981.

"Cumberland Presbyterian Church Vertical File." Williamson County Archives, Franklin, TN.

Daniel, Pete. "The Convict Lease War." *Tennessee Historical Quarterly* (Fall 1975).

Daniel, Susan. *Cemeteries and Graveyards of Rutherford County, Tennessee*. Murfreesboro, TN: Rutherford County Historical Society, 2005.

Dickson, R. J. *Ulster Emigration to Colonial America, 1718–1775*. London: Routledge & Kegan Paul, 1966.

Doyle, David Noel. *Ireland, Irishmen, and Revolutionary America, 1760–1820*. Dublin: Published for the Cultural Relations Committee of Ireland by Mercier Press, 1981.

Dunaway, Wayland F. *The Scotch-Irish of Colonial Pennsylvania*. Hamden, CT: Archon Books, 1962.

Durham, Walter T. *Before Tennessee: The Southwest Territory, 1790–1796*. Piney Flats, TN: Rocky Mount Historical Association, 1990.

_____. "Kasper Mansker: Cumberland Frontier." *Tennessee Historical Quarterly*, Vol. XXX, No. 2 (Summer 1971): 154–177.

Eller, Ronald D. *Miners, Millhands, and Mountaineers: Industrialization of the Appalachian South, 1880–1930*. Knoxville, TN: University of Tennessee Press, 1982.

Ely, James W. Jr., ed. *A History of the Tennessee Supreme Court*. Knoxville, TN: The University of Tennessee Press, 2002.

Eslinger, Ellen. *Running Mad for Kentucky*. Lexington, KY: University of Kentucky Press, 2004.

"Estimable Woman Dies in Oklahoma." *Nashville Banner*, November 19, 1908.

Finger, John R. *Tennessee Frontiers: Three Regions in Transition*. Bloomington: Indiana University Press, 2001.

_____. "Tennessee Indian History: Creativity and Power." *Tennessee Historical Quarterly* 54 (Winter 1995): 286–305.

Foote, Shelby. *The Civil War: A Narrative, Red River to Appomattox*. New York: Vintage Books, 1986.

Fulcher, Richard Carlton. *1780–1790 Census of the Cumberland Settlements: An Enumeration of the Inhabitants of Record in Davidson County, Being at Times in North Carolina, and the Territory South of the River Ohio*. Brentwood, TN: February 1, 1979.

Fulton, Eleanore Jane, and Barbara Kendig Mylin. *An Index to the Will Books and Intestate Records of Lancaster County, Pennsylvania 1729–1850*. Baltimore, MD: Genealogical Publishing Co. Inc., 1974.

Gamble, Bonnie L. "The Nashville, Chattanooga and St. Louis Railroad, 1845–1880: Preservation of a Railroad Landscape." M.A. Thesis, Middle Tennessee State University, 1993.

Gaston, Kay Baker. "George Dickel Tennessee Sour Mash Whiskey: The Story Behind the Label." *Tennessee Historical Quarterly* 57 (1998): 150–167.

Golden, Claudia, and Frank D. Lewis. "The Economic Cost of the American Civil War: Estimates and Implications." *Journal of Economic History*, Vol. 35, No. 2 (June 1975): 299–326.

"Governor Buchanan Talks." *New York Times*, December 11, 1891, p. 2.

Grigg, David B. *Population Growth and Agrarian Change: An Historical Perspective.* Cambridge, England: Cambridge University Press, 1980.

Hansen, John Mark. *Gaining Access: Congress and the Farm Lobby, 1919–1981.* Chicago, IL: University of Chicago Press, 1991.

Hart, Roger L. *Redeemers, Bourbons, and Populists: Tennessee, 1870–1896.* Baton Rouge, LA: Louisiana State University Press, 1975.

Haywood, John. *The Civil and Political History of the State of Tennessee.* Knoxville, TN: Tenase Co., 1823, 1969.

Henderson, Archibald. *The Conquest of the Old Southwest.* Seattle, WA: The Wide World School, 2001.

Herr, Kincaid A. *The Louisville and Nashville Railroad 1850–1940, 1941–1959.* Louisville, KY: *L&N Magazine*, 1959.

History of Homes and Gardens of Tennessee, 1936. Garden

Study Club of Nashville Collection. Tennessee State Library and Archives, Nashville, TN. Accession Number: 95-062, Date Completed: October 4, 1995, Location: I-E-7, Stack #2 and the Map Cases.

Hoffman, Carol. "John Price Buchanan, Farmer and Politician." *Rutherford County Historical Society Publication*, No. 21 (Summer 1983).

Holloway, Margaret Endsley. "The Reaction in Tennessee to the Federal Elections Bill of 1890." M.A. Thesis, University of Tennessee, December 1970.

Hopkinson, Patty. "The Buchanan Estate Scam," *Buchanan Banner*, Vol. 25 (4), Winter 1997, *http://www.geocities. com/genealogist@sbcglobal.net/scam.html*.

Howard, Patricia B. "World War II." *Tennessee Encyclopedia of History & Culture*, ed. Carroll Van West. Nashville, TN: Rutledge Hill Press, 1998: 1080–1084.

Hurst, Rebekah. "Noah's All-American Star: Coffee County Is Home to Women's Basketball Legend Alline Banks-Sprouse." *Manchester Times*, September 5, 2007, pp. 1A, 5A.

"Inquiry Fails to Unearth Trace of Buchanan Estate." *Houston Chronicle*, January 20, 1932.

Interview with James M. Buchanan Jr., December 1, 2006, Blacksburg, VA.

Interview with James M. Buchanan Jr., May 16, 2007, Indianapolis, IN.

James Buchanan's October 1987 lecture at Trinity University. *http://www.trinity.edu/nobel.*

Jamison, Robert David. *Letters and Recollections of a Confederate Soldier, 1860–1865.* Nashville, TN: H. D. Jamison, 1964.

Johns, E. K. *Deed Abstracts on Stones River from Deed Books A, B, C, D, E, F* of *Davidson County, Tennessee, 1784–1806.* Murfreesboro, TN: Rutherford County Historical Society, 1981.

Johnson, Charles. *City behind a Fence: Oak Ridge, Tennessee, 1942–1946.* Knoxville, TN: University of Tennessee Press, 1981.

Johnson, Leland, and Daniel Schaffer. *Oak Ridge National Laboratory: The First Fifty Years.* Knoxville, TN: University of Tennessee Press, 1994.

Johnston, William Preston. *The Life of General Albert Sidney Johnston.* New York: D. Appleton & Co., 1878.

Jones, John B. Jr. "Convict Lease Wars." *Tennessee Encyclopedia of History and Culture,* ed. Carroll Van West, *http://tennesseeencylopedia.net/.*

Jones, Robert B. III. *Tennessee at the Crossroads: The*

State Debt Controversy, 1870–1883. Knoxville, TN: University of Tennessee Press, 1977.

Klein, Phillip Shriver. *President James Buchanan: A Biography.* University Park, PA: Pennsylvania State University Press, 1962.

Kyriakoudes, Louis M. *The Social Origins of the Urban South: Race, Gender, and Migration in Nashville and Middle Tennessee, 1890–1930.* Chapel Hill, NC: University of North Carolina Press, 2003.

Lancaster County, Pennsylvania Will Book I, 1–5; B, 1–457.

Lauder, Kathy. Adopted from the historical research of Nancy Helt and Joseph Wilson. "A History of the Buchanan Log House," *http://pages/prodigy.net/nhn.slate/nh0090.html*, retrieved December 16, 2008.

Lester, Connie L. "Disenfranchising Laws." *Tennessee Encyclopedia of History & Culture*, ed. Carroll Van West. *http://tennesseeencyclopedia.net*.

_____. "Farmers' Alliance." *The Tennessee Encyclopedia of History and Culture*, ed. Carroll Van West, *http://tennesseeencyclopedia.net*.

_____. *Up from the Mudsills of Hell: The Farmers' Alliance, Populism, and Progressive Agriculture in Tennessee, 1870–1915.* Athens, GA: University of Georgia Press, 2006.

Mancini, Matthew J. *One Dies, Get Another: Convict Leasing in the American South, 1866–1928.* Columbia, SC: University of South Carolina Press, 1996.

Martin, Jennifer. "On the National Register: Campus School Complex Dates from 1929." *Murfreesboro Post,* *http://www.murfreesboropost.com/news.php?viewStory =2871*, retrieved July 30, 2007.

Mayhew, Anne. "A Reappraisal of the Causes of Farm Protest in the United States, 1870–1900." *Journal of Economic History*, Vol. 32, No. 2 (June 1972): 464–475.

McDonnold, B. W. *History of the Cumberland Presbyterian Church*, 4th ed. Nashville, TN: Board of Publication of Cumberland Presbyterian Church, 1899.

McKenzie, Robert Tracy. *One South or Many? Plantation Belt and Upcountry in Civil War-Era Tennessee.* New York: Cambridge University Press, 2002.

Middle Tennessee State Normal School *Bulletin.* Middle Tennessee State University Special Collections. Middle Tennessee State University, Murfreesboro, TN.

Milady in Brown. Belmont University Library Special Collections. Belmont University, Nashville, TN.

Minute Book, Rutherford County Chancery Court, August 21, 1869. Rutherford County Archives, Murfreesboro, TN.

Minute Book, Rutherford County Chancery Court, April Term 1876. Rutherford County Archives, Murfreesboro, TN.

Minute Book, Rutherford County Chancery Court, April 3, 1877. Rutherford County Archives, Murfreesboro, TN.

Minute Book, Rutherford County Chancery Court, May 31, 1877. Rutherford County Archives, Murfreesboro, TN.

Moore, Wayne C. "Paths of Migration." In *First Families of Tennessee: A Register of Early Settlers and Their Present Day Descendants*. Knoxville, TN: East Tennessee Historical Society, 2000.

Nashville Banner. Vol. XVI, No. 82 (July 16, 1891): 1.

Nashville Banner. Vol. XVI, No. 84 (July 18, 1891): 1.

Nashville Banner. Vol. XVI, No. 86 (July 21, 1891): 1.

Nashville Banner. Vol. XVI, No. 87 (July 22, 1891): 1.

Nashville Banner. Vol. XVI, No. 89 (July 24, 1891): 1.

Nashville Banner. Vol. XVI, No. 90 (July 25, 1891): 1.

Nashville Banner. Vol. XVII, No. 101 (August 1, 1892): 1.

Nashville Banner. Vol. XVII, No. 106 (August 6, 1892): 1.

Nashville Banner. Vol. XVII, No. 107 (August 10, 1892): 1.

Nashville Banner. Vol. XVII, No. 113 (August 15, 1892): 1.

Nashville Banner. Vol. XVII, No. 114 (August 16, 1892): 2.

National Bureau of Economic Research, "NBER Macrohistory, VIII Income and Employment," *http://www.nber.org/databases/macrohistory/contents/chapter08.html*, retrieved August 23, 2010.

Obituary of Thomas Buchanan, *Review Appeal*, Vol. XCVI, No. 22 1 (November 12, 1908).

Partlow, Thomas E. *Sugg's Creek Cumberland Presbyterian Church: An Early History*. Lebanon, TN: Thomas E. Partlow, 1974.

Phillips, Margaret I. *The Governors of Tennessee*. Gretna, LA: Pelican Publishing Company, 1978.

Pittard, Homer. *The First Fifty Years*. Murfreesboro, TN: Middle Tennessee State College, 1961.

Pittard, Mabel. *Rutherford County*. Memphis, TN: Memphis State University Press, 1984.

Prospectus, Belmont College for Young Women. Belmont University Library Special Collections, Nashville, TN.

Putnam, A. W. *History of Middle Tennessee or Life and*

Times of Gen. James Robertson. Knoxville, TN: University of Tennessee Press, 1971.

Ralph, Mrs. Robert. "History of Mt. Tabor Cumberland Presbyterian Church Begins in 1836." Rutherford County Historical Society.

Ransom, Roger, and Richard Sutch. "The Impact of the Civil War and Emancipation on Southern Agriculture." *Explorations in Economic History*, Vol. 12 (1975): 1–28.

Records of Davidson Court, Vol. B. Tennessee State Library and Archives, Nashville, TN.

Records of Davidson Court, Vol. C. Tennessee State Library and Archives, Nashville, TN.

Records of the State of North Carolina, Vol. XXIX: 571–573.

Rutherford County Tax Records, 1877–1878. Rutherford County Archives, Murfreesboro, TN.

Satz, Ronald N. *Tennessee's Indian Peoples: From White Contact to Removal, 1540–1840.* Knoxville, TN: University of Tennessee Press, 1979.

Shapiro, Karin A. *A New South Rebellion: The Battle Against Convict Labor in the Tennessee Coalfields, 1871–1896.* Chapel Hill, NC: University of North Carolina Press, 1998.

Shiflett, Crandall A. *Coal Towns: Life, Work, and Culture in the Company Towns of Southern Appalachia, 1880–1960*. Knoxville, TN: University of Tennessee Press, 1991.

Sims, Carlton, ed. *A History of Rutherford County*. Murfreesboro, TN.: Carlton C. Sims, 1947.

Sloan, Eugene. *With the Second Army Somewhere in Tennessee*. Murfreesboro, TN: Middle Tennessee State College, 1956.

Smith, G. Herbert. "A Letter from Kentucky." *Mississippi Valley Historical Review*, Vol. 19, No. 1 (June 1932).

Speer, William S. *Sketches of Prominent Tennesseans*. Nashville, TN: Albert B. Tavel, 1888.

Spence, John C. *Annals of Rutherford County, Volume Two: 1829–1870*. Nashville, TN: Williams Printing Company, 1991.

State Records of North Carolina. Walter Clark, ed., Vol. XIX, 1782–1784.

Temin, Peter. "The Post-Bellum Recovery of the South and the Cost of the Civil War." *Journal of Economic History*, Vol. 36, No. 42 (December 1976): 898–907.

Tennesseans in the Civil War, Part I: A Military History of the Confederate and Union Units with Available Rosters of Personnel. Nashville, TN: Tennessee Historical Commission, 1964.

Thirtle, Colin, David Schimmelpfennig, and Robert F. Townsend. "Induced Innovation in United States Agriculture, 1880–1990: Time Series Tests and an Error Correction Model." *American Journal of Agricultural Economics*, Vol. 84 (August 2002): 598–614.

Treasurer's and Comptroller's Papers, Revolutionary War Pay Vouchers. State of North Carolina, Department of Cultural Resources.

The War of the Rebellion: A Compilation of the Official Records of the Union and Confederate Armies. Series I, Vol. VII.

U.S. National Park Service, Civil War Soldiers and Sailors System Database. *http://www.itd.nps.gov/cwss/*.

Warwick, Rick. *Freedom and Work in the Reconstruction Era: The Freedman's Bureau Labor Contracts of Williamson County, Tennessee.* Heritage Foundation of Franklin and Williamson County, TN, 2006.

_____. *Williamson County, The Civil War Years Revealed through Letters, Diaries, and Memoirs.* Franklin, TN: The Heritage Foundation of Franklin and Williamson County, 2006.

Weeks, Terry. *Heart of Tennessee: The Story and Images*

of Historic Rutherford County. Murfreesboro, TN: Courier Printing Co., 1992.

Wells, O. V. "The Depression of 1873–79." *Journal of Farm Economics*, Vol. 19, No. 2 (May 1937): 621–633.

Winters, Donald L. *Tennessee Farming, Tennessee Farmers.* Knoxville, TN: University of Tennessee Press, 1994.

Williams, Samuel Cole. *Tennessee during the Revolutionary War.* Knoxville, TN: University of Tennessee Press, 1974.

Williamson County Court Minutes. Vol. 12. Williamson County Archives, Franklin, TN.

Williamson County, Tennessee, Deed Book L. Williamson County Archives, Franklin, TN.

Wright, Gavin. "Cotton Competition and the Post-Bellum Recovery of the American South." *Journal of Economic History*, Vol. 34, No. 3 (Sept. 1974): 610–635.

FIGURES

1. Lancaster County Townships and Boroughs, p. 27, courtesy *LancasterHistory.org*.

2. Family tree for the first three Buchanan generations, p. 28.

3. Wilderness Road, p. 31, Tennessee State Library and Archives Collection, from *Daniel Boone & the Wilderness Road*, 1910, p. 341, Library Collection.

4. Fort Nashborough, p. 36, Tennessee State Library and Archives, Library Collection, image 1490, negative 607, Drawer 7, Folder 210.

5. Major John Buchanan portrait, p. 39, Tennessee State Library and Archives, Portrait Collection 1700–1960, Tennessee State Museum Portrait No. 183; Tennessee State Library Image no. 19464, TSLA RG 197.

6. Buchanan Station, p. 41, Tennessee State Library and Archives, Garden Study Club of Nashville Collection, 95-062.

7. Major John Buchanan's *Arithmetic*, p. 44, Tennessee State

Library and Archives, Tennessee Historical Society miscellaneous collection, I-A-1v, B-238, T-100.

8. Buchanan Family Cemetery in Cool Springs, TN, p. 66, courtesy of Reuben Kyle.

9. 47th General Assembly of the State of Tennessee, 1886–1888, p. 114, Tennessee State Library and Archives, Tennessee General Assembly, Composite Photograph Collection, RG 211.

10. Governor John Price Buchanan, p. 121, Tennessee State Library and Archives, Portrait Collection 1700-1960, RG 197, Box 1, Volume 1.

11. James Shannon Buchanan, p. 162, University of Oklahoma, Western History Collections, Photographic Collection, Sardis Roy Hadsell Collection, HADSELL 39.

12. Panorama View, Kingfisher College, p. 164, University of Oklahoma, Western History Collections, Oklahoma Postcard Collection, 1290.

13. Buchanan Family picture circa 1986, p. 181, courtesy Jeff Buchanan.

14. Homer Pittard Campus School, Murfreesboro, p. 182, © Middle Tennessee State University.

15. Nobel Prize in Economic Science, p. 202, © ® The Nobel Foundation.

16. James M. Buchanan Jr., p. 207, George Mason University.

INDEX

Agricultural Wheel, *110*
Battle of the Bluff, *37*
Battle of Buchanan Station, *40*
Belmont College, *167, 168*
Buchanan, Alexander, *37, 38*
Buchanan Arithmetic, *3, 43, 44, 161*
Buchanan cemetery, *66, 71, 72*
Buchanan Station, *40, 41, 42, 43, 46, 66*
Buchanan, James McGill, *176*
Buchanan, James McGill Jr., *5, 7, 8, 13, 50, 143, 177, 206, 207, 212*
Buchanan, James Shannon, *75, 161, 162, 163, 166*
Buchanan, John Price, *3, 13, 23, 75, 77, 82, 89, 95, 96, 105, 107, 110, 111, 112, 113, 114, 115, 116, 117, 118, 121, 125, 127, 128, 136, 140, 141, 143, 161, 162, 166, 175, 185*
Buchanan, John Senior, 27, 28, 29, 34, 35, 38, 45, 67
Buchanan, John III, 66, *71*
Buchanan, Major John, *28, 35, 37, 38, 39, 42, 43, 44, 45, 48, 65, 66, 161*
Buchanan, origins of name, *23, 24*
Buchanan, Thomas, *67, 75, 76, 77, 78, 79, 81, 84, 85, 86,*

87, 88, *161, 167, 175, 185*
Calculus of Consent, The, 1, 199, 241, 243
Civil War, *75, 77, 78, 82, 91, 96, 105, 106, 107, 109, 115, 117, 124, 127*
Coal Miners' Strike, *127*
Constitutional economics, *205, 238, 239, 240, 244*
Cumberland Compact, *34, 165*
Cumberland Presbyterian Church, *115, 163, 183, 185*
Farmers' Alliance, *111, 112, 113, 114, 115, 116, 117, 118, 119, 121, 122, 124, 125, 129, 132, 135, 136, 137, 138*
George Mason University, *8, 201, 206*
Knight, Frank, *11, 18, 197*
McGill, James, *90, 91, 93, 94, 95*
Middle Tennessee State University, *5, 43, 171, 175, 181, 207*
Nobel Prize, *4, 6, 7, 11, 19, 143, 165, 197, 201, 206, 207, 244, 255*
People's Party, *138, 139, 140*
Public Choice, *1, 5, 8, 199, 200, 201, 202, 203, 206, 238, 240, 250, 252, 253*
Ridley, Sarah (Sally), *39, 40, 42, 43, 66*
Tullock, Gordon, *1, 199, 201, 241, 243*
University of Chicago, *1, 5, 10, 11, 15, 18, 163, 197, 198, 199*
University of Oklahoma, *75, 162, 163, 164, 176*
University of Virginia, *1, 11, 198, 200*
Virginia Tech, *201*
Wicksell, Knut, *10, 240*
Wilderness Road, *30, 31, 34, 37*
Williamson County, *ii, 28, 65, 66, 67, 71, 75, 76, 77, 78, 79, 80, 81, 82, 84, 86, 88, 89, 120, 185, 212*

APPENDIX A.

THE POLITICAL ECONOMY OF JAMES M. BUCHANAN

At this point in the narrative, James Buchanan may take up his own story. The material that follows is posed as answers to a series of questions regarding his work with responses drawn from his own writings and a few segues provided by the author to clarify the transition between one source and another. The indented answers to the questions are in James Buchanan's own words, and each quotation is followed by a citation of the source. Unless otherwise indicated, the citations are for works authored solely by James M. Buchanan. Any material contained in brackets was added by the author. The questions and materials were chosen for their accessibility to readers who are not economists: no graphs, no mathematics, and a minimum of technical economic jargon. Although the material may still prove challenging to many readers, it should afford some insight into the basic premises of Buchanan's work.

A typical modern textbook definition of economics might be "the study of how *societies choose* to allocate scarce

economic resources among alternative uses." What is James Buchanan's definition?

> *Economists "should" concentrate their attention on a particular form of human activity, and upon the various institutional arrangements that arise as a result of this form of activity. Man's behavior in the market relationship, reflecting the propensity to truck and to barter, and the manifold variations in structure this relationship can take; these are the proper subjects for the economist's study.*

Source: "What Should Economists Do?" *Southern Economic Journal* 30 (January 1964), pp. 213–222.

The term *constitutional economics* is often associated with public choice and specifically with your work. What is *constitutional economics*, and how does it differ from more traditional economics?

> *[Constitutional] economics is fundamentally concerned with the framework for social processes, that is, the structure of and interrelationships among political and economic institutions, all of which are designed to allow people, individually and collectively, to pursue desired ends. The underlying theory of constitutional economics is a theory of the rules by which political and economic processes will be allowed to operate through time.*

Source: Richard B. McKenzie, "Introduction," Richard B. McKenzie (ed.), *Constitutional Economics*, Lexington,

MA: Lexington Books, 1984, p. 1.

> *In any observed and ongoing poker game, individuals, as players, abide by the rules that exist and that define the game itself. Players adopt this or that strategy in attempts to win within the existing rules. At the same time, however, the same persons may evaluate the rules themselves, and they may enter into side discussions about possible changes in the rules so as to make for a "better" game. If, as a result of such discussion, agreement is reached, then rules are changed and the regime shifts. A new constitution emerges.*

Source: "The Ethics of Constitutional Order," *Essays on the Political Economy*, Honolulu: University of Hawaii Press, 1989. Reprinted in *The Complete Works of James M. Buchanan, Vol. 1, The Logical Foundations of Constitutional Liberty*, p. 369.

> *[Constitutional economics versus orthodox economics:] in the latter individuals make choices among alternatives with constraints imposed exogenously. Constitutional economics directs analytical attention to the choice among constraints.*
>
> *It is essential to acknowledge ... that individuals choose to impose constraints or limits on their own behavior, primarily ... as part of an "exchange."*

Source: *The Economics and the Ethics of Constitutional Order*, Ann Arbor, MI: University of Michigan Press, 1991, p. 5.

What role does unanimity or full consensus play in constitutional economics?

> At this point, I introduce the great Swedish economist Knut Wicksell, who is the most important of all precursory figures in public choice, especially for my own work and for what we now call "constitutional economics." In his dissertation published in 1896, Wicksell was concerned about both the injustice and the inefficiency of untrammeled majority rule in parliamentary assemblies. . . . Majority rule seemed quite likely to impose net costs or damages on large segments of the taxpayer-beneficiary group. Why should members of such minorities, facing discrimination, lend their support to political structures? Unless all groups can somehow benefit from the ultimate exchange with the government, how can overall stability be maintained?
>
> Wicksell proposed that the voting rule be modified in the direction of unanimity. If the agreement of all persons in the voting group should be required to implement collective action, then this result, in itself, would guarantee that all persons secure net gains and, further, that the projects so approved yield, overall, benefits in excess of costs.
>
> Wicksell recognized that, if applied in a literal voting setting, a requirement of unanimity would produce a stalemate, since it allows each and every person to play off against all others in the group. Such a recognition, however, does not change the value of the unanimity

> rule as a benchmark for comparative evaluation. In suggestions for practical constitutional reforms, Wicksell supported changes in voting rules from simple to qualified majorities, perhaps, for example, the requirement of five-sixths approval for collective proposals.

Source: *http://www.pubchoicesoc.org/about_pc.html*, retrieved November 28, 2006.

Majority rule is one of the touchstones of modern democracy. How does majority rule pose a problem in your analysis?

> *[Majority] rule has been elevated to the status which the unanimity rule should occupy. At best, majority rule should be viewed as one among many practical expedients made necessary by the costs of securing widespread agreement on political issues when individual and group interests diverge. (p. 96)*

> *A central feature of our analysis is the demonstration that the operation of simple majority rule, quite independently of any assumption about individual motivation, will almost always impose external cost on the individual. (p. 145)*

Source: Buchanan and Tullock, *The Calculus of Consent*.

Please elaborate on how economics, as most readers might understand it, enters this analysis of constitutions.

One of the great advantages of an essentially economic approach to collective action lies in the implicit recognition that "political exchange," at all levels, is basically equivalent to economic exchange. (p. 248)

Insofar as participation in the organization of a community, a State, is mutually advantageous to all parties, the formation of a "social contract" on the basis of unanimous agreement becomes possible. (p. 248)

Conceptually, men can reach agreement on rules, even when each party recognizes in advance that he will be "coerced" by the operation of agreed-on rules in certain circumstances. A potential thief, recognizing the need for protecting his own person and property, will support laws against theft, even though he will anticipate the probability that he will himself be subjected to punishment under these laws. (p. 249)

[In the case of economic exchange the parties have conflicting interests. The potential buyer wishes to pay the lowest possible price while the potential seller wishes to receive the highest possible price. But those differences are resolved when the actual exchange occurs. In the case of the social contract, the issues are more complex, but] . . . *the central notion of mutuality of gain may be carried over to the political relationship. (pp. 250–251)*

The only test for the presence of mutual gain is agreement. (p. 251)

[There may be times when agreement on the social contract is not possible.] Under such conditions societies will tend to be controlled by some groups which will tyrannize over other groups. (p. 251)

Source: Buchanan and Tullock, *The Calculus of Consent*.

Another term you use to describe your methodology is *contractarian*. Could you explain that term?

[The English philosopher] John Locke and all of the writers who were responsible for developing the conception of "natural rights" made much of the distinction between the constitutional decision, which determines the rules for collective action, and the operational decision, which determines the shape of collective action within previously chosen rules. The individual, possessing certain inherent or natural rights, enters into a contractual relationship with his fellows, a relationship that is expressed in a constitution. The subsequent obligation of the individual to abide by the decisions made by the collectivity, so long as these are reached constitutionally, lies in his obligation to fulfill the contract once made.

Source: Buchanan and Tullock, *The Calculus of Consent*, p. 314.

How are we, your readers, to compare your approach and method of analysis to those of other scholars?

Constitutional economics is a domain of inquiry and discourse among scientists who choose to perceive social interaction as a set of complex relationships, both actual and potential, among autonomous persons, each of whom is capable of making rational choices. The domain, as such, cannot be extended to include inquiry by those who choose to perceive social interaction differently.... These [different] visions are, indeed, alternative "windows" on the world. And the process through which individuals choose among such windows remains mysterious. How can empirical evidence be made convincing when such evidence must, itself, be perceived from only one vantage point at a time? The naiveté of modern empirical economists in this respect verges on absurdity.

Source: "The Domain of Constitutional Political Economy," *The Economics and the Ethics of Constitutional Order*, Ann Arbor, MI: University of Michigan Press, 1991, p. 18.

Does this mean we cannot compare the economics of James Buchanan with the economics of, say, Kenneth Arrow, another Nobel Prize winner in economics?

The underlying normative economics of Buchanan and Arrow cannot be directly compared since their whole perspective differs.... The strictly positive elements of analysis are, of course, the same.

Source: Author's correspondence with James M. Buchanan, December 4, 2006.

For many years economics was known as the queen of the social sciences, but in recent decades some economists stake the claim that economics is a science. Can economics be a science?

> *I suggest that we think of the role of the economist, and of economic science, in terms analogous to that of the ordinary natural scientist, and of natural science. Think then of the natural scientist not as a discoverer of new laws of nature and the universe, not as someone who is continually expanding the boundaries of what we know about the natural environment, but instead, as a human repository of knowledge about the natural environment, as it is now known to exist. Think, that is, of the noncreative natural scientist, and of the role of such a person, and of science, in society.*
>
> *What does such a scientist do? As a rough cut of an answer, consider the definition of the natural or physical feasibility space. The scientist draws the boundaries between what is and what is not feasible given the known constraints of the physical universe. . . . The predictions of natural science tell us what we can and cannot do with the materials and potential forces that exist. (pp. 31–32)*
>
> *If economics is to be compared with natural science, economists should be able to define what can and cannot be done with the human materials and potential that exist. Economists, and economic science, should generate a feasibility space, fully analogous to that generated*

> *for the physical universe by natural science. (p. 32)*

> *Economists are frequently accused of committing the naturalist fallacy, the derivation of an "ought" from an "is." ... If the economists can observe politically motivated action aimed quite explicitly at the achievement of results that are clearly beyond the boundaries of feasibility, given the existing regime, no norms are violated when and if they call attention to this as scientific fact. (p. 41)*

Source: "There Is a Science of Economics," *Post-Socialist Political Economy: Selected Essays*, Cheltenham, U.K.: Edward Elgar, 1997, pp. 9–19. Reprinted in *The Collected Works*, Vol. 12, pp. 30–43.

Economists distinguish between positive and normative economics. Positive economics is the study of what is, while normative economics is the study of what ought to be. The first is seen to be scientific and the second prescriptive. Some have accused you of offering normative for positive economics. How do you respond to this?

> *Critics have charged that my work has been driven by an underlying normative purpose, and, by inference, if not directly, they have judged me to be mildly subversive. . . . [Anyone] who models interaction structures that might be is likely to be accused of biasing analysis toward those alternatives that best meet his personal value standards. . . . I shall acknowledge that I work always within a self-imposed constraint that some may*

choose to call a normative one. I have no interest in structures of social interaction that are nonindividualist . . . That is to say, I do not extend my own analysis to alternatives that embody the rule of any person or group of persons over other persons or groups of persons. If this places my work in some stigmatized normative category, so be it.

Source: "From the Inside Looking Out," *Better Than Plowing*, p. 152.

What is the basis for your preference for a minimalist government?

Much of what we have observed in modern politics is best described as action taken without understanding, or even consideration, of the rules that define the constitutional order. I have referred to this politics as "constitutional anarchy," by which I mean a politics that is almost exclusively dominated by, and derivative from, the strategic choices made by competing interests in disregard for the effects on political structures. This politics has emerged into its current position because we, as citizens, have failed to discharge our ethical obligations. We have behaved as if the very structure of our social order, our constitution defined in the broadest sense, will remain invariant or will, somehow, evolve satisfactorily over time without our own active participation.

Simple observation of the behavior of our political

and judicial agents should indicate that such a faith is totally without foundation. We may, of course, continue to default on the ethical obligation of constitutional citizenship. If we do so, however, we leave unchecked the emerging tyranny of the nonconstrained state, a tyranny that can be dislodged only with revolution. Neither such tyranny nor its consequent revolution is necessary if we, as individuals, can recover, even in part, the ethical principle upon which our constitutional order is established.

We must attend to the rules that constrain our rulers, and we must do so even if such attention may not seem to be a part of a rational choice calculus. The amorality of acquiescence generates despair and longing; the morality of constitutional understanding embodies hope as a necessary complement. (p. 157)

Source: "The Ethics of Constitutional Order," *The Economics and Ethics of Constitutional Order*, (Ann Arbor, MI: University of Michigan Press, 1991), pp. 153–157.

What can a person be predicted to do when the external institutions force upon him a role in a community that extends beyond his moral-ethical limits? The tension shifts toward the self-interest pole of behavior; moral-ethical principles are necessarily sublimated. The shift is exaggerated when a person realizes that others in the extended community of arbitrary and basically amoral size will find themselves in positions comparable to his own. How can a person act polit-

> *ically in other than his own narrowly defined self-interest in an arbitrarily sized nation of more than 200 million? Should we be at all surprised when we observe the increasing usage of the arms and agencies of the national government for the securing of private personal gain?*

Source: "Markets, States, and the Extent of Morals," *American Economic Review*, Vol. 68 (May 1978), pp. 364–368. Reprinted in *The Logical Foundations of Constitutional Liberty, Collected Works, Vol. 1*, p. 365.

> *It is in this setting . . . that the natural forces that generate the Leviathan state emerge and assume dominance. With no overriding principle that dictates how an economy is to be organized, the political structure is open to maximal exploitation by the pressures of well-organized interests which seek to exploit the powers of the state to secure differential profits. The special-interest, rent-seeking, churning state finds fertile ground for growth in this environment.*

Source: "Socialism Is Dead but Leviathan Lives On," The John Bonython Lecture, CIS Occasional Paper 30 (Sydney: Centre for Independent Studies, 1990), pp. 1–9. Reprinted in *The Logical Foundations of Constitutional Liberty, Collected Works, Vol. 1*, p. 186.

You have written a great deal on taxation and the limitation of the power of government to tax. What would you recommend regarding the ability of government to tax?

For the ordinary citizen, the power to tax is the most familiar manifestation of the government's power to coerce. This power to tax involves the power to impose, on individuals and private institutions more generally, charges that can only be met by a transfer to government of economic resources, or financial claims to such resources. . . . [The] power to "tax" is simply the power to "take."

Source: Geoffrey Brennan and James M. Buchanan, *The Power to Tax: Analytical Foundations of a Fiscal Constitution, Vol. 9, The Complete Works of James M. Buchanan*, p. 11.

A central message of public choice theory tells us that if politics generates undesirable results, it is better to examine the rules than to argue about different policies or to elect different representatives. . . . What is wrong with things as they are? And among any extended listing that each of us might make, which of the observed results might be amenable to fixing through changes in the rules?

Fiscal irresponsibility stares us in the face and cries out for correction. . . . Political leaders, both legislative and executive, with public support, act as if it is possible to spend without taxing, indeed as if the fisc offers the political equivalent of perpetual motion.

Source: James M. Buchanan, "Three Amendments: Responsibility, Generality, and Natural Liberty," *Cato Unbound*, December 5, 2005, *http://www.cato-unbound.*

org/2005/12/05/james-m-buchanan/three-amendments, retrieved August 22, 2012.

> *[We] . . . recommend that the Constitution of the United States be amended so as to include the following provisions:*
> 1. *The president shall be required to present annually to Congress a budget that projects federal outlays equivalent to federal revenues.*
> 2. *The Congress, both in its initial budgetary review, and in its subsequent approval, shall be required to act within the limits of a budget that projects federal outlays equivalent to federal revenues. (There is, of course, no requirement that the congressional budget be the same as that submitted by the president.)*
> 3. *In the event that projections prove in error, and a budget deficit beyond specified limits occurs, federal outlays shall be automatically adjusted downward to restore projected balance within a period of three months. If a budget surplus occurs, funds shall be utilized for retirement of national debt.*
> 4. *Provision of this amendment shall be made fully effective within five years of its adoption. To achieve an orderly transition to full implementation, annual budget deficits shall be reduced by not less than 20 percent per year in each of the five years subsequent to the adoption of the amendment. Departure from this 20-percent rule for annual adjustment downward in the size of the deficit shall be treated in the same manner as departure from budget balance upon full implementation.*

> 5. *Provisions of this amendment may be waived only in times of national emergency, as declared by two-thirds of both houses of Congress, and approved by the president. Declarations of national emergency shall expire automatically after one year.*

Source: James M. Buchanan and Richard E. Wagner, *Democracy in Deficit: The Political Legacy of Lord Keynes*, Vol. 8, *The Complete Works of James M. Buchanan*.

At times there has been controversy concerning public choice and public choice scholars. Can you elaborate?

> *Cynical descriptive conclusions about behavior in government threaten to undermine the norm prescribing public spirit. The cynicisms of journalists—and even the writings of professors—can decrease public spirit simply by describing what they claim to be its absence. Cynics are therefore in the business of making prophecies that threaten to become self-fulfilling. If the norm of public spirit dies, our society would look bleaker and our lives as individuals would be more impoverished. That is the tragedy of "public choice." [Emphasis added.]*

Source: Steven Kelman, "'Public Choice' and Public Spirit," *Public Interest*, Vol. 87, No. 80 (1987), pp. 93–94.

> *Public choice theory has been widely touted as being defined by the attribution of Homo economicus motivations to actors in their political roles. Homo*

economicus — the wealth-maximizing egoist — should be seen to play no more significant a role in public choice analysis than in the whole program of economic theory more generally. And it is simply wrong to conceive of economics as nothing more than egoistic psychology. (p. 80)

Public choice — the hardheaded, realistic, indeed cynical model of political behavior — can be properly defended on moral grounds if we adopt a "constitutional perspective" — that is, if the purpose of the exercise is conceived to be institutional reform, improvements in the rules under which political processes operate. The perspective requires that we shift attention away from the analysis of policy choice by existing agents within existing rules, and towards the examination of alternative sets of rules. (p. 87)

Source: Geoffrey Brennan and James M. Buchanan, "Is Public Choice Immoral? The Case for the 'Nobel' Lie," *Virginia Law Review*, Vol. 74, No. 2, *Symposium on the Theory of Public Choice* (March, 1988), pp. 179–189. Reprinted in *The Collected Works of James M. Buchanan*, Vol. 13, *Politics as Public Choice*, Part 2, *Public Choice and Its Critics*, pp. 79–89.

Many people would describe your positions on economics and the political order as *conservative*, **yet the title of your 2005 book is** *Why I, Too, Am Not a Conservative: The Normative Vision of Classical Liberalism*. **Could you clarify this distinction?**

The title for [the] book ...refers to one of F. A. Hayek's most famous essays "Why I am not a conservative."... Hayek felt that it was necessary to stake a claim for identification as a classical liberal and, in doing so, forestall the co-option of the term "liberal" by those who would subvert the time-tested emphasis on individual liberty itself. For Hayek, for whom socialism remained his lifelong bete noir, *conservative bedfellows were welcome enough, but he saw no reason to crawl under the terminological blanket. (p. 1)*

Conservatism and liberalism are two distinct ways of looking at and thinking about the whole realm of human interaction, or, even more fundamentally, at the human beings who interact one with another. (p. 1)

Etymologically, the word "conservative" implies that positive value is placed on "that which is," whether this be behavioral practices, conventions, traditions, moral standards, coordination rules or economic, social or political institutions (including constitutional structures). And also, "that which is" describes the assignment of persons to separate roles as subjects, rulers, principals or agents. By inference, the burden of proof is placed on those who advocate change.

The conservative assigns a value privilege to the status quo, as such. The classical liberal may recognize that the status quo is privileged by the fact of its existence, but there is no independent positive value assigned. The liberal is willing to examine alternatives without surmounting the threshold that the conservative places between what is and what might be. (p. 2)

Confusion arises from the distinction between the classical and the American modern liberal in their expressed attitudes toward the dividing line between collective and private action, that is, between the state and the market. In the setting of the late twentieth and early twenty-first centuries, the classical liberal tends to oppose extensions of state or collective authority—extensions that often command the support of the American modern liberal. In this stance on policy, the classical liberal joins forces with the conservative who seeks to preserve the existing division of authority. As politically organized, the classical liberal and the conservative forces seem to share basic values when, in fact, their positions rest on very different foundational attitudes. (p. 5)

Source: Why I, Too, Am Not a Conservative: The Normative Vision of Classical Liberalism, Northampton, MA: Edward Elgar Publishing, 2005.

You have observed that "if Jim Buchanan can win the Nobel Prize, anyone can." Could you explain why you feel that way?

It is, I think, safe to say that my selection in 1986 gave hope and encouragement to more people than most other awards, and certainly more than any other previous award in economics. Here was Jim Buchanan, a country boy from Middle Tennessee, educated in rural public schools and a local public teachers college, who is not associated with an establishment university, who has never shared the academically fashionable soft left ideology, who has worked in totally unorthodox subject matter with very old-fashioned tools of analysis, chosen by a distinguished and respected Swedish committee. It was not at all surprising that the sycophants for the orthodoxies, in both ideas and institutions, were shocked and dismayed. And it is indeed gratifying to me that members of the "great unwashed," the unorthodox of many disciplines, looked on me as the representative embodiment of that which might be.

Source: "At the Turn of a Half-Century," *Better Than Plowing*, pp. 35–36.

APPENDIX B.

BUCHANAN FAMILY GENEALOGY

The following family genealogy is not intended to be complete or guaranteed to be 100 percent accurate. However, the authors have included only information they are reasonably confident is correct. We have no conclusive evidence of the generations before John Buchanan Senior or his date of birth or birthplace. Perhaps the genealogical records available through *Ancestry.com* might resolve those questions, but we offer that suggestion with the caveat that the persons listed may not be the correct ones for the family in this book. We invite any reader to offer additions or corrections to the family record provided here.

1. JOHN BUCHANAN, birth year and place uncertain, died 1787 in Mill Creek, Davidson County, TN. He married JANE TRINDLE, daughter of WILLIAM TRINDLE and MARGARET. She was born in 1743 in Lancaster County, PA.

    Children of JOHN BUCHANAN and JANE TRINDLE:
    i. SARAH JANE BUCHANAN, b. 05 Nov 1755, Lancaster, Lancaster County, PA; d. 1802, Stones River

Homes, Rutherford County, TN, m. JAMES TODD, 17 Sep 1777, Lancaster County, PA.
   ii. ALEXANDER BUCHANAN, b. 1758, Lancaster, Lancaster County, PA; d. 02 Apr 1781, French Lick, TN. Killed in the Battle of the Bluffs.
   iii. MAJOR JOHN BUCHANAN, b. 12 Jan 1759, Harrisburg, Dauphin County, PA; d. 07 Nov 1832, Mill Creek, Nashville, TN.
   iv. SAMUEL BUCHANAN, b. 1760, Harrisburg, Dauphin County, PA; d. 1787, Mill Creek, Nashville, TN.
   v. NANCY BUCHANAN, b. 1762, Harrisburg, Dauphin County, PA; d. 18 Apr 1856, Nashville, TN; m. JAMES MULHERRIN.

2. SARAH JANE BUCHANAN, b. 05 Nov 1755, Lancaster, Lancaster County, PA; d. 1802, Stones River Homes, Rutherford County, TN, m. JAMES TODD, 17 Sep 1777, Lancaster County, PA.

Children of SARAH JANE BUCHANAN and JAMES TODD:
   i. MARY POLLY TODD, b. 28 Jun 1778, Virginia.
   ii. NANCY TODD, b. 2 Aug 1780, Cumberland Settlement, TN.
   iii. JAMES B. TODD, b. 5 Sep 1783, Nashville, Davidson County, TN.
   iv. JENNIE TODD, b. 1786, Buchanan Station, Davidson County, TN.
   v. ESTHER TODD, b. 1788, Buchanan Station, Davidson County, TN.
   vi. REBECCA TODD, b. 2 Mar 1790, Buchanan Station, Davidson County, TN.

vii. ELIZABETH TODD, b. 1792, Buchanan Station, Davidson County, TN.

viii. JAMES MULHERRIN TODD, b. 7 Jul 1795, Buchanan Station, Davidson County, TN.

ix. SARAH TODD, b. 1798, Buchanan Station, Davidson County, TN.

2. MAJOR JOHN BUCHANAN was born 12 Jan 1759 in Harrisburg, Dauphin County, PA, and died 07 Nov 1832 in Mill Creek, Nashville, TN. He married (1) MARGARET KENNEDY, daughter of JOHN KENNEDY and MARGARET ROWAN, in 1786. She was born in about 1763 in Harrisburg, Dauphin County, PA, and died 15 May 1787 in Nashville, TN. He married (2) SARAH RIDLEY, daughter of GEORGE RIDLEY and ELIZABETH WEATHERFORD, 15 Oct 1791 in Nashville, Davidson County, TN. It is claimed that she was born 28 Nov 1773 in Watauga Valley, TN, but there is no documentation of her birth. She died 23 Nov 1831 in Nashville, TN.

Child of JOHN BUCHANAN and MARGARET KENNEDY:

i. JOHN BUCHANAN, b. 15 May 1787, Nashville, Davidson County, TN; d. 29 Jun 1834, Franklin, Williamson County, TN.

Children of JOHN BUCHANAN and SARAH RIDLEY:

ii. GEORGE BUCHANAN, b. 11 Oct 1792, Mill Creek, Davidson County, TN; d. 22 Feb 1816, Mill Creek, Davidson County, TN.

iii. ALEXANDER BUCHANAN, b. 23 Mar 1794, Mill Creek, Davidson County, TN; d. 18 Apr 1836, Davidson

County, TN; m. MARY RIDLEY.

iv. ELIZABETH BUCHANAN, b. 29 Dec 1795, Buchanan Station, Davidson County, TN; d. 08 May 1875, Nashville, Davidson County, TN; m. THOMAS H. EVERETT, 01 Nov 1810.

v. SAMUEL BUCHANAN, b. 27 Aug 1797, Buchanan Station, Davidson County, TN; d. 20 Feb 1816, Davidson County, TN.

vi. WILLIAM BUCHANAN, b. 12 Jan 1800, Buchanan Station, Davidson County, TN; d. 21 Jan 1849; m. JANE E. HOGAN.

vii. JANE TRINDLE BUCHANAN, b. 23 Mar 1802, Buchanan Station, Davidson County, TN; d. 06 May 1837, Old Jefferson, Rutherford County, TN; m. GEORGE GOODWIN.

viii. JAMES BRYANT BUCHANAN, b. 10 Mar 1804, Buchanan Station, Davidson County, TN; d. 06 Jul 1862, Davidson County, TN; m. LETTIE ROBERTS.

ix. MOSES RIDLEY BUCHANAN, b. 04 Apr 1806, Buchanan Station, Davidson County, TN; d. 30 May 1887, Mill Creek, Davidson County, TN; m. SARAH V. RIDLEY, 16 Jul 1827.

x. SARAH VINCENT BUCHANAN, b. 31 Dec 1807, Buchanan Station, Davidson County, TN; d. 10 Apr 1866, Davidson County, TN; m. JAMES A. WILLIAMS.

xi. CHARLES BINGLEY BUCHANAN, b. 28 Oct 1809, Mill Creek, Davidson County, TN; d. 16 Apr 1836, Davidson County, TN.

xii. RICHARD GREGORY BUCHANAN, b. 03 Nov 1811, Buchanan Station, Davidson County, TN; d. Memphis, Shelby County, TN; m. MARTHA A.

MURPHEY.

xiii. HENRY RIDLEY BUCHANAN, b. 08 Nov 1814, Buchanan Station, Davidson County, TN; d. 1898, Nashville, Davidson County, TN.

xiv. NANCY MULHERRIN BUCHANAN, b. 31 Jul 1818, Buchanan Station, Davidson County, TN; d. 18 Jul 1881; m. (1) HENRY BRIDGES; m. (2) JACKSON SMITH.

2. NANCY BUCHANAN, b. 1762, Harrisburg, Dauphin County, PA; d. 18 Apr 1856, Nashville, TN; m. JAMES MULHERRIN.

Child of NANCY BUCHANAN and JAMES MULHERRIN:
i. CHARLES MULHERRIN Jr., b. 1785, Nashville, Davidson County, TN.

3. JOHN BUCHANAN was born 15 May 1787 in Nashville, Davidson County, TN, and died 29 Jun 1834 in Franklin, Williamson County, TN. He married MARGARET SAMPLE, daughter of ROBERT SAMPLE and ANN BETTS, 19 Sep 1805 in Davidson County, TN. She was born 1791 in Buckingham Township, Bucks County, PA, and died 29 Sep 1860 in Williamson County, TN.

Children of JOHN BUCHANAN and MARGARET SAMPLE:
i. JOHN SAMPLE BUCHANAN, b. 06 Apr 1806; d. 30 May 1868, Gibson, TN; m. ELIZABETH VAUGHAN, 01 Nov 1827.

Children of JOHN SAMPLE BUCHANAN and ELIZABETH VAUGHAN:

a. JOHN BUCHANAN.
b. MARY MARGARET BUCHANAN.
c. WILLIAM THOMAS BUCHANAN.
d. JACK BUCHANAN.

ii. MARGARET ANN BUCHANAN, b. 05 Dec 1807; d. 31 May 1868; m. SMITH H. SAMPLE, 24 Feb 1825.

Children of MARGARET ANN BUCHANAN and SMITH H. SAMPLE:
a. JOHN B. SAMPLE.
b. SARAH ANN SAMPLE.
c. DANIEL J. SAMPLE.
d. MARGARET B. SAMPLE.
e. SUSAN J. SAMPLE.
f. THORNTON S. SAMPLE.
g. ELLEN M. SAMPLE.
h. MARY M. SAMPLE.
i. CALCEDONIA RACHEL SAMPLE.

iii. WILLIAM M. BUCHANAN, b. 20 Apr 1809, Davidson, TN; d. 31 May 1880, Franklin, Williamson County, TN.

Children of WILLIAM M. BUCHANAN:
a. THOMAS E. BUCHANAN.
b. ELIZABETH MARGARET BUCHANAN.
c. MARY JANE BUCHANAN.
d. HENRY BUCHANAN.
e. EVALINE BUCHANAN.
f. JOHN E. BUCHANAN.

g. GEORGE R. BUCHANAN.
h. EPHRIAM BUCHANAN.
i. CHARLES BUCHANAN.
j. SUSAN BUCHANAN.

iv. SAMUEL BUCHANAN, b. 20 Nov 1810; d. May 1825.
v. SARAH BUCHANAN, b. 20 Mar 1812; d. 22 May 1873; m. DANIEL I. SAMPLE, 1830, and JOHN H. STONE.
vi. ELIZABETH BUCHANAN, b. 01 Aug 1815, TN; d. 22 Jun 1892, Woodbury, Cannon County, TN; m. LEMUEL BETHELL, 11 Dec 1833, Franklin, Williamson County, TN.

Children of ELIZABETH BUCHANAN and LEMUEL BETHELL:
a. PALMYRA A. BETHEL.
b. WILLIAM R. E. BETHEL.
c. MARY ANN JORDAN BETHEL.
d. MARGARET B. BETHEL.
e. SARAH TENNESSEE BETHEL.
f. INDIANA C. BETHEL.
g. LYDIA HALL BETHEL.
h. TOMMIE B. BETHEL.
i. JOHN BETHEL.
j. BUCHANAN BETHEL.

vii. ROBERT S. BUCHANAN, b. 03 Feb 1818; d. 14 Jun 1883, Franklin, Williamson County, TN; m. HARRIET S. BATEMAN, 08 Feb 1836.

Children of ROBERT S. BUCHANAN and HARRIET S.

BATEMAN:
a. JOHN BUCHANAN.
b. ENOCH B. BUCHANAN.
c. THOMAS S. BUCHANAN.
d. ROBERT BUCHANAN.
e. WILLIAM BUCHANAN.
f. MAGGIE BUCHANAN.
g. DANIEL C. BUCHANAN.
h. VIRGINIA C. BUCHANAN.
i. BETTIE BUCHANAN.
j. MAY BUCHANAN.
k. SYDNEY BUCHANAN.
l. SUSIE BUCHANAN.

viii. MARY BRANDON BUCHANAN, b. 17 Jul 1820, Franklin, Williamson County, TN; m. GEORGE GOODWIN.
ix. THOMAS BUCHANAN, b. 21 Jan 1823, Williamson County, TN; d. 24 Oct 1908, Norman, OK.

4. THOMAS BUCHANAN was born 21 Jan 1823 in Williamson County, TN, and died 24 Oct 1908 in Norman, OK. He married REBECCA JANE SHANNON 05 Nov 1846 in Franklin, Williamson County, TN, daughter of JAMES SHANNON and MARY GRAY. She was born 19 Jan 1829 in Williamson County, TN, and died 12 Oct 1882 in Franklin, Williamson County, TN.

Children of THOMAS BUCHANAN and REBECCA JANE SHANNON:
i. JOHN PRICE BUCHANAN, b. 24 Oct 1847, Williamson, TN; d. 14 May 1930, Murfreesboro, Rutherford

County, TN; m. FRANCIS LOUISE MCGILL, 24 Oct 1867; b. 30 Oct 1848, Murfreesboro, Rutherford County, TN; d. 30 Nov 1927, Murfreesboro, Rutherford County, TN.
ii. JAMES SHANNON BUCHANAN, b. 14 Oct 1864, Franklin, Williamson County, TN; d. Mar 1930, Norman, Cleveland County, OK; m. (1) KATHRYN OSTERHAUS; m. (2) VINNIE GALBRAITH, 24 Jun 1896, Norman, Cleveland County, OK; d. 15 May 1921.
iii. MARY MARGARET BUCHANAN, b. 20 Jul 1849, TN; d. 10 May 1913.
iv. JENNIE THOMAS BUCHANAN, b. 16 Jan 1863; d. 18 Nov 1908, Norman, Cleveland County, OK.
v. SUSAN ANN BUCHANAN, b. 12 Sep 1851; m. GEORGE ISHAM MATTHEWS; b. 01 Mar 1846, TN.

5. JOHN PRICE BUCHANAN was born 24 Oct 1847 in Williamson County, TN, and died 14 May 1930 in Murfreesboro, Rutherford County, TN. He married FRANCIS LOUISE MCGILL, daughter of JAMES MCGILL and AMANDA NORMAN, 24 Oct 1867. She was born 30 Oct 1848 in Murfreesboro, Rutherford County, TN, and died 30 Nov 1927 in Murfreesboro, Rutherford County, TN.

Children of JOHN BUCHANAN and FRANCIS MCGILL:
i. REBECCA JANE BUCHANAN, b. 1876, TN; d. 23 Jun 1965, Murfreesboro, Rutherford County, TN.
ii. ROBERT NORMAN BUCHANAN, b. Jun 1878, TN.
iii. MAGGIE D. BUCHANAN, b. 01 Nov 1880, TN; d. 13 Jul 1900.

iv. SUSIE M. BUCHANAN, b. Jul 1883, TN; d. 1928.
v. FRANCES L. BUCHANAN, b. Nov 1885, TN; d. about 1967; m. NEWT WEBB.
vi. THOMAS BUCHANAN, b. 25 Nov 1869, Rutherford County, TN; d. 13 Jun 1908, Murfreesboro, Rutherford County, TN; m. LILY RAMSEY, 24 Oct 1895, Marshall County, TN.
vii. JAMES MCGILL BUCHANAN, b. 20 Sep 1888, Rutherford County, TN; d. 24 Jul 1979, Murfreesboro, Rutherford County, TN.
viii. JOHN PRICE BUCHANAN JR., b. Aug 1873, Rutherford County, TN; d. about 1963.

6. ROBERT NORMAN BUCHANAN was born Jun 1878 in Tennessee. He married MAGGIE TERRY.

Children of ROBERT BUCHANAN and MAGGIE TERRY:
i. ROBERT NORMAN BUCHANAN JR.
ii. MARGARET TERRY BUCHANAN.
iii. THOMAS BUCHANAN.

7. SUSIE M. BUCHANAN was born Jul 1883 in Tennessee and died 1928. She married CLIFT MOORE EPPS about 1908 in Tennessee. He was born 29 Jun 1885 in Tennessee and died 06 Nov 1958 in Tom Green County, TX.

Children of SUSIE Buchanan and CLIFT EPPS are:
i. CLIFT M. EPPS, b. 1909, Texas.
ii. LAWRENCE EPPS, b. 1911, Tennessee.
iii. FRANCES EPPS, b. 1914, Tennessee.

8. JAMES MCGILL BUCHANAN was born 20 Sep 1888 in Rutherford County, TN, and died 24 Jul 1979 in Murfreesboro, Rutherford County, TN. He married LILA HERRIN SCOTT 30 Apr 1918, daughter of THOMAS SCOTT and ANNIE MARSHALL. She was born 14 Dec 1889 in Davidson County, TN, and died 11 Feb 1953 in Murfreesboro, Rutherford County, TN.

Children of JAMES BUCHANAN and LILA SCOTT:
i. JAMES MCGILL BUCHANAN JR., b. 03 Oct 1919, Rutherford County, TN, d. 09 Jan 2013, Blacksburg, VA; m. ANN BAKKE, 05 Oct 1945, San Francisco, CA; b. 21 Aug 1909; d. 14 Nov 2005.
ii. LILA SCOTT BUCHANAN, b. 1923.
iii. ELIZABETH BUCHANAN, b. 1933, Rutherford County, TN.

Notes

Sources include Thomas Buchanan, 1898, Davidson County, TN—Biographies—Buchanan Family, "History of the Buchanan Family," *http://files.usgwarchives.org/tn/davidson/bios/bchnan01.txt*, accessed July 17, 2012. If the family had 10 children, one is obviously missing from the list, possibly one who died in childhood.

See also Eleanore Jane Fulton, Barbara Kendig Mylin, *An Index to the Will Books and Intestate Records of Lancaster County, PA, 1729–1850: With an Historical Sketch and Classified Bibliography* (Google eBook).

CPSIA information can be obtained at www.ICGtesting.com
Printed in the USA
LVOW10*0249110914

403510LV00003B/17/P